"Few (if any) books so compassionately and constructively address the common, under-addressed overlap between adult attention deficit/hyperactivity disorder (ADHD) and anxiety. I imagine anyone living with ADHD will benefit from reading *The Adult ADHD and Anxiety Workbook*."

—**Mark Bertin, MD**, author of *Mindful Parenting for ADHD* and
Mindfulness and Self Compassion for Teen ADHD

"Practical, concise, compact. Gets straight to the point, nothing fancy, no dillydallying. In other words, eminently ADHD-friendly. Written by a man who understands ADHD deeply, as well as anxiety in its many forms. Artful in combining narrative with workbook exercises, this book will entertain you, educate you, and give you practical ways to design and enhance your life. A superb, helpful book written by one of the masters in the field."

—**Edward "Ned" Hallowell, MD**, author and coauthor of numerous books,
including *Driven to Distraction* and *ADHD Explained*

"*The Adult ADHD and Anxiety Workbook* takes the overwhelm and confusion out of learning to manage ADHD. Ramsay takes the reader, step by doable step, chapter by chapter, guiding them to whittle their challenges down to size, giving them clear actions to take to manage their ADHD."

—**Kathleen Nadeau, PhD**, internationally known author of more than a
dozen books on ADHD; and founder and director of The Chesapeake
Center, one of the largest private ADHD specialty clinics in the US

"J. Russell Ramsay has written a terrific workbook for individuals with adult ADHD—which is also valuable for family members, therapists, and others who want to help. People with ADHD tend to become very overwhelmed with the demands of everyday life. But the step-by-step process outlined in this workbook teaches you not only how to cope, but also how to motivate yourself to take each step."

—**Judith S. Beck, PhD**, president of the Beck Institute for Cognitive
Behavior Therapy, and author of *Cognitive Behavior Therapy*

T0287105

"This useful book does not provide simple general answers to get rid of anxiety. Instead, it invites the reader to personalize the text by writing into the workbook specific examples of ways their daily life with ADHD is currently complicated by various types of anxiety in different situations. Ramsay describes strategies and specific behaviors which can be useful gradually to reduce excessive anxiety despite the 'consistent inconsistency' of ADHD."

—**Thomas E. Brown, PhD**, clinical professor of psychiatry and neuroscience at the University of California, Riverside School of Medicine

"Ramsay's latest book is a much-needed guide full of important information about living with ADHD and anxiety, taking readers through an introspective and practical journey toward self-improvement. For anyone who has read other books on ADHD but were missing this crucial component—the connection between ADHD and anxiety—this book is for you!"

—**Abigail Levrini, PhD**, licensed psychologist; and author of the American Psychological Association bestseller, *Succeeding with Adult ADHD* and *ADHD Coaching*

"As if coping with ADHD weren't challenging enough, you're grappling with anxiety, too? Ramsay is a leading clinical expert on adult ADHD who deeply understands the challenges. Dive into this real-world workbook and benefit from the proven cognitive behavioral therapy (CBT) tools that he codeveloped. Ramsay doesn't just offer advice. He coaxes you into practical, game-changing strategies. Get ready to boost your confidence, focus, and calm."

—**Gina Pera**, author of *Is It You, Me, or Adult A.D.D.?* and coauthor of *Adult ADHD-Focused Couple Therapy*

"Tailored for those navigating ADHD and anxiety, Ramsay's workbook offers practical strategies, empowering exercises, and insightful guidance. Gain control over cognitive distortions, enhance focus, and conquer challenges with proven techniques. Written with empathy and expertise, this workbook is your companion on the journey to a more fulfilling and balanced life."

—**Stephanie Moulton Sarkis, PhD**, psychotherapist, and author of *Gaslighting* and *Healing from Toxic Relationships*

"In his wonderful new book, J. Russell Ramsay shows us why ADHD and anxiety are deeply intertwined, and what people can do to replace old coping strategies with more effective ones. Applying key concepts from CBT, the book is threaded with many helpful reflection exercises and practice opportunities to develop practical strategies and personal insights to manage a wide range of anxiety-related issues. I'll be recommending this terrific book to adults with ADHD and those professionals who work with them!"

—**Sharon Saline, PsyD**, author of the award-winning book, *What Your ADHD Child Wishes You Knew* and *The ADHD Solution Card Deck*

"Delve into the intricacies of anxiety and ADHD with this essential guide! This book is a must-read, offering valuable insights and actionable strategies for those navigating the challenges of anxiety and ADHD. I wholeheartedly recommend it as an indispensable tool for personal growth and resilience."

—**Tamara Rosier, PhD**, author of *Your Brain's Not Broken*

"ADHD rarely travels alone, and anxiety is one of its more common companions. This book is a masterful and compassionate guide for clinicians and patients alike on how to navigate the combination of ADHD and anxiety together. Ramsay's vast experience of working with adults with ADHD shines through the book, and makes it one of the best resources on the topic. I highly recommend it!"

—**Lidia Zylowska, MD**, psychiatrist, and author of *The Mindfulness Prescription for Adult ADHD* and *Mindfulness for Adult ADHD*

"ADHD expert Russell Ramsay delivers to ADHD adults a clear and actionable set of practices to help mitigate the chaos of executive function impairments and anxiety. Readers will find a friendly and wise companion in Ramsay's voice, as he speaks compassionately, authentically, and directly—with a touch of humor—in a realistic manner without being cynical, and encouraging without being falsely saccharine."

—**Scott Spradlin**, cofounder of Wichita DBT at NorthStar Therapy, and author of *Don't Let Your Emotions Run Your Life*

The Adult ADHD *&* Anxiety WORKBOOK

Cognitive Behavioral Therapy Skills to
Manage Stress, Find Focus, *and* Reclaim Your Life

J. Russell Ramsay, PhD

New Harbinger Publications, Inc.

Publisher's Note

NEW HARBINGER PUBLICATIONS is a registered trademark of New Harbinger Publications, Inc.

New Harbinger Publications is an employee-owned company.

The adapted "Outline Your Antiprocrastination Plan," "Stay Motivated with Your Antiprocrastination Plan," and "Define-Your-Role Strategy Steps" practices are Copyright © 2020 by American Psychological Association. Reproduced and adapted with permission. The official citation that should be used in referencing this material is Ramsay, J. R. (2020). *Rethinking Adult ADHD: Helping Clients Turn Intentions into Action.* American Psychological Association. No further reproduction or distribution is permitted without written permission from the American Psychological Association.

Cover design by Amy Shoup

Acquired by Jess O'Brien

Edited by Elizabeth Dougherty

Printed in the United States of America

26   25   24

10   9   8   7   6   5   4   3   2

Contents

Foreword

I tell clients and presentation audiences that if you have ADHD and you're not at least a little anxious and depressed, then you're not paying attention.

Okay, that's a joke—and it's also painfully true. If you're reading this, then you know what I'm talking about. If you're not managing your ADHD well, you will probably have more setbacks, disappointments, frustrations, and just plain situations where you didn't do what you planned to. Or at least hoped to. I wish I could say that feeling anxious or depressed was just your imagination running wild with negative ideas, but you know that there is too much of a seed of truth to those doubts and uncomfortable feelings. That's the bad news.

Here's the good news. Just as poorly managed ADHD can make it really easy to feel anxious, getting on top of your ADHD makes it a whole lot easier to legitimately have less to worry about. This is really important if you saw a therapist or took medication for anxiety before you were diagnosed with ADHD. Hopefully it was somewhat helpful, but it never worked as well as you would have hoped, did it? It's kind of like painting the water stains on the ceiling but not fixing the leak in the roof. All it takes is yet another ADHD moment for all those bad feelings to come flooding back in again.

That's what is so great about this book. It's chock-full of strategies to help you actually get more done and (equally important) then feel good about it. ADHD is fundamentally a neurological condition, but there is a ton of psychology that develops from a lifetime of ADHD moments. Not only is it harder to consistently do the right things at the right times, but it also becomes harder to give yourself credit for what you are doing. Or to believe that you're up for the challenge in the first place.

I can't think of a better person to write this book than Russ Ramsay, PhD. He is the epitome of the clinician/researcher—he knows how to work directly with people and he knows all the research that guides the most effective interventions. I always learn something from his writing and presenting and I quote him all the time in my presentations. He's really good at integrating what others have found, adding his own insights, and explaining it in a way that makes sense.

Cognitive behavioral therapy is the perfect method to break the ADHD/anxiety pipeline. It can reduce the impact of ADHD on your daily life and also give you the tools to bounce back from those situations that go sideways. If you put in the effort, you will feel better for it.

Russ knows that the goal isn't to have less ADHD or anxiety; it's to have more of a life. This means making better use of your time, chipping away at procrastination, making your relationships more satisfying, handling the inevitable setbacks resiliently, and making the time to take good care of yourself. This is what will empower you to pursue what is really important to you. That's the final payoff and you deserve it.

—Ari Tuckman, PsyD
    Author of four books on ADHD: *ADHD After Dark*;
    Understand Your Brain, Get More Done; *More Attention, Less Deficit*;
    and *Integrative Treatment for Adult ADHD*

INTRODUCTION

Feeling Emotionally Overwhelmed by Life

You're most likely reading this book because you are an adult with attention deficit/hyperactivity disorder (ADHD) who is also experiencing anxiety. I'm calling this the *adult ADHD–anxiety connection*. I see its effects often in my work as a psychologist treating adults with ADHD, and we'll explore it in depth in this workbook. My hope is that the proven cognitive behavioral therapy (CBT) tools in this book will help you better manage your co-occurring ADHD and anxiety, so you can feel more confident, focused, and calm. This is a workbook, so you will have many opportunities to practice applying these tools to your specific situation.

Common Scenarios

To start, let's look at some common scenarios that you may relate to. In each story, an adult experiences both ADHD and anxiety. (All client examples are disguised and composites of different cases to protect confidentiality.)

Barry's Story

Barry is a late-twentysomething man who was diagnosed with ADHD in college. He's wrestled with organization and follow-through problems all his life. He had hoped that after college he'd be better able to stay on top of things in a job where he was paid and with projects that had significance beyond grades. Unfortunately, ADHD continued to create troubles for him. His levels of stress and anxiety rose along with his increased adult responsibilities, both inside and outside the office.

When his work struggles led to a mediocre performance review, Barry reached out to me for help with ADHD. One of our early sessions addressed an important work report that Barry had forgotten about until just before our Friday meeting. This was characteristic of the problems that led him to me. He had until Monday to finish it, a tight but doable timeframe. We drew up what he agreed was a reasonable plan to face this straightforward project. He figured he'd knock the report out in two hours or so. I asked Barry, "What could interfere with carrying out your plan?" Barry said, "I know I can do it, but ugh! I can see myself stressing out all weekend and waiting until the last minute to do it. I'll get it done, but then I'll worry about how it could have been better had I started earlier."

And that's what happened.

Does this sound familiar? Do you make plans for yourself that you put off way too long and pay the price later? These could be tasks for work or school, or even daily matters like household chores, errands, or anything effortful that seems like work. That expectation of having to expend effort on something the opposite of fun or interesting is what makes any task more prone to procrastination (Jaffe 2013), especially for adults with ADHD.

You've no doubt heard lots of advice about planning and organizing your time and responsibilities, but you also know what a challenge that is as an adult with ADHD. Even thinking about plans can be anxiety-provoking and stressful. Maybe you feel overwhelmed by the stress of juggling a seemingly relentless onslaught of unavoidable duties. You may feel like even getting one thing done requires so much time, focus, and energy that if you did it, you would then feel too exhausted and stressed to take on anything else. What's more, adults with ADHD often find themselves repeatedly apologizing and scrambling to make amends. They may even fabricate excuses for lateness to avoid disappointing others.

Kelly's Story

Being disorganized, apologizing, and scrambling to make amends are some of the challenges Kelly, who had long struggled with ADHD, faced. Kelly's disorganization compromised her ability to keep promises, make it to scheduled events, and take care of other day-to-day responsibilities. Kelly fought back tears in a session recounting her "snack shame" incident. For the second time in a row, she had forgotten her turn as designated snack-bringer for her daughter's soccer game. Because she was already late, she dropped off her daughter and raced off in search of a convenience store—only to get pulled over for speeding. Kelly had tried and discarded innumerable planning systems and finally had resigned herself to winging it each day.

However, each day left her exhausted with nagging worries that she'd missed something important and would later learn how she disappointed someone.

How often have you faced those dope-slap moments when you suddenly realize you've forgotten something important, like Kelly's snack shame? Apart from those out-of-the-blue panicked moments, are your everyday stresses of contending with your adult duties and roles affecting others, like your family, friends, or coworkers? This is the public-facing aspect of ADHD. The ripple effects of ADHD-related difficulties add stress when you're already dealing with people's reactions when you arrive late, forget a promise, miss an important detail, misplace something, or experience any similar snags. You've probably encountered disapproving looks, heavy sighs, and outright criticisms.

On the other hand, do you sometimes feel unappreciated or misunderstood? Does it seem like your positive attributes and deeds are overlooked? Maybe you feel stressed and on the defensive, trying hard to please others. Efforts, such as spending inordinate time and energy on straightforward tasks but still falling behind, may present itself as perfectionism. You might identify ways other people could help you but hold back asking because you're worried that you'll appear high maintenance and that they'll dismiss your requests. Susan faced these issues.

Susan's Story

Susan, who has ADHD, found what appeared to be a good-fit job in sales. Her vibrant personality made her a customer favorite, especially with those she met face-to-face. However, following up with clients by phone or email stressed her out. Due to her anxieties, Susan typically let phone calls go to voicemail and put off replying to emails. She worried that her difficulties organizing and expressing her thoughts made her seem scattered and amateurish in her communications. Consequently, Susan spent a disproportionate amount of time crafting emails and repeatedly "getting ready to get ready" to return voicemails. Susan knew she needed help but hesitated to speak up, nervous that her asking would come across as whining. She felt she needed to simply get over it.

Do you stress about what others think of you, that is, your reputation? Maybe you feel like you can be yourself around certain people, which can be a stress buffer. Maybe you don't have a safe harbor of supportive people who get you. Even if you have good friends, you might worry that you'll be rejected for some reason, even though there is no hint of that happening now. Maybe it happened to you before. Nevertheless, a lifetime of criticisms, teasing, or disappointments and frustrations from ADHD can erode your sense of self. This drop in confidence makes you less willing to trust connections with others, which is something Trent faced.

Trent's Story

Trent, an amiable and likable man, described feeling on the defensive with anyone at work or in his personal life who was not in his innermost circle. His stress stemmed from his long-standing distractibility and mind-wandering that affected him in classes, meetings, conversations, and other social situations. Trent became adept at masking his ADHD-caused space-outs, biding time until he regained the conversation thread. In doing so, though, he often missed important details, including directions at work. He described his mindset as bracing himself, ever on guard for potential disapproval.

Trent's first therapist diagnosed him with social anxiety disorder, assuming his reticence indicated a classic, inordinate fear of being judged negatively by others. After some initial progress, Trent plateaued before discovering that ADHD was driving his anxieties. It was then that Trent learned of rejection sensitive dysphoria (Dodson 2023). Rejection sensitive dysphoria is essentially strong emotional reactions to feeling rejected or criticized that are disproportionate in their degree and durability, even if there is some truth to the matter. We will discuss it in greater detail later in the book.

Trent's initial anxiety diagnosis makes some sense. Anxiety is the most common coexisting emotional diagnosis seen with adult ADHD. If you have both anxiety and ADHD, ADHD is likely the chief source of your anxiety. You may not experience extreme or debilitating anxiety, like panic attacks or agoraphobia, but you probably have instances similar to Barry's procrastination and ugh feeling, Susan's self-doubt and worries, or Trent's bracing. Or, like Kelly, you feel the overwhelm of disorganization, but the solution of committing to planning your day sparks even worse apprehension. It's these sorts of difficulties that led them to seek help.

The Adult ADHD and Anxiety Workbook can help you address these and other issues that stem from having ADHD and anxiety in your life. The challenges of living with ADHD are magnified by stress and anxiety—a super sized double whammy of worry and life problems. In fact, many people first seek help for anxiety or depression and only later discover that ADHD was the missing puzzle piece.

Perhaps you were diagnosed with ADHD in childhood. Some still view it as a childhood diagnosis, but it is now known to persist into adulthood for most children and teens with the diagnosis. If you were diagnosed as a child, you may have taken medications or taken steps like sacrificing sleep and extracurriculars to keep up with school. You may have also benefited from structure that others provided, such as parents helping you with homework. The responsibilities and roles of adulthood are less forgiving. There is no end of school year where you start anew with a clean slate. Things change in adulthood, with many strategies that worked in school being unsustainable in a job or college. You're not only trying to get yourself through the day, but others, such as children or employers, also depend on you. This adds another layer of responsibilities, stress, and frustration. You also must manage finances, maintain a living space, and keep and organize commitments, such as doctor visits and social events.

On the other hand, you may have gone through childhood and adolescence with some combination of distractibility, restlessness, and poor impulse control and resultant problems. You may have struggled with problems such as disorganization, late assignments, or forgetfulness. You may have sensed that you weren't fulfilling your potential or that something was off but not had it identified as ADHD until adulthood.

In your earlier life, you may have gotten by or even did quite well. That may have changed when you began to face the multiple, persistent demands of adulthood that demand good organizational skills. Also, ADHD treatment tools and structures that parents or teachers maintained are now up to you to implement alone, which can feel like trying to tie your shoes while running full speed. Hopefully, you now know that your struggle with procrastinating, getting to places on time, keeping up with children's schedules, and having poor follow-through on plans isn't due to lack of desire or capability, but due to ADHD.

No doubt, you can cite countless examples of how some assortment of inattention, restlessness, and impulsivity caused problems for you. But these symptoms alone don't capture the essence of ADHD. Using a medical example, they're like having a fever but not knowing what malady is causing it. In this view, ADHD is chiefly an issue of chronic, wide-ranging problems and unreliability with self-regulation.

Self-Regulation

Self-regulation is the suite of behaviors that you use to manage yourself. It's your capacity for self-control, which helps you to do whatever it is you set out to do (Goldstein and Naglieri 2014). It's what helps you turn your intentions into actions that move you forward in achieving goals, big and small. If you've ever woken up to an alarm you set, you've exerted self-regulation. If you've ever set an item by your front door so that you remember to take it with you to work the next day, that's self-regulation. Have you ever deleted a social media app to avoid wasting time on it? That's self-regulation.

You also practice self-regulation through your mindset. For example, you may focus on the delayed payoffs when preparing slides for a work presentation or exercising when you didn't feel like it. These long-range motivations can be incentivized in the short-term, such as waiting to watch a movie until after finishing your slides or workout.

Everybody has these self-regulation capacities, which are also known as *executive functions* (Barkley 2012; 2015). Executive functions can be broken down into skill categories, which chapter 1 will list in more detail. These include time management; follow-through on plans; organization, such as keeping track of your stuff, like keys and work IDs; and organization duties, like keeping up with finances and car registrations.

The issue with ADHD is that the executive functions are chronically unreliable. For instance, you might put off preparing your slides until the morning of your work presentation due to your stress at the thought of organizing them. Or you might convince yourself that watching a movie now will put you in the mood to exercise later.

When thinking about the problems you face that led you to this book, you probably used the language of executive-function problems relevant to your life, such as procrastinate less, organize your days better, respond to friends and family quicker, keep up with bills and chores, and be less sensitive to others' reactions. Procrastination, which chapter 5 covers in detail, causes problems that leave you stressed and frustrated but still dealing with its ripple effects. Similarly, lateness, missed meetings, and forgotten promises from poor time management create stress and anxieties in relationships and other areas of life.

Can you see how ADHD itself creates anxiety due to executive-function problems? From your experiences growing up with ADHD, stress, apprehension, and other guises of anxiety become associated with your various life roles and endeavors. Anxiety signals the risk that comes with the "consistent inconsistency" of ADHD. Most adults with ADHD have a history of frustrations that create stress. Coping with ADHD itself is stressful. Encountering your consistent inconsistency activates anxiety. In turn, anxiety promotes a desire to escape or avoid whatever is making you anxious, which is called *escape-avoidance*. This pattern magnifies and is magnified by ADHD, like gasoline on fire. You don't work on your slides, even though you know it's better to be prepared. Or you skip your gym trip to watch a movie, even though you know you'd have felt better had you gone.

Your adult ADHD–anxiety connection is triggered by the day-in and day-out demands of organizing and keeping up with your roles and responsibilities, all while contending with the difficulties posed by ADHD. You're probably juggling many adult roles and responsibilities. In addition to time management at work, you may have a shared custody and visitation schedule with an ex-spouse. You may taxi aging parents to medical visits on top of attending night school and keeping up your apartment. You might find your eyes periodically filling with tears from equal parts fatigue and stress caused by dealing with ADHD all day, every day. This overwhelm is stoked by the uncertainty and self-doubt that result from persistent difficulties with poor self-regulation. This creates a vicious, self-perpetuating cycle of frustrations that you likely feel powerless to do anything about. This is where ADHD and anxiety become fused.

If any of this sounds like you and what you're facing, this workbook will help you. It will provide skills that will make a difference in your day-to-day life, help turn your intentions into actions, and help you rise above stress and anxiety.

Everyone has felt levels of stress, anxiety, and other unpleasant feelings that made us avoid carrying out a plan despite knowing we'd feel more stressed later. Hence, this workbook is all about implementation—helping you do whatever it is that you set out to do!

How This Book Can Help You

I offer you this workbook, first and foremost, as a psychologist who specializes in adult ADHD. I practice cognitive behavioral therapy (CBT). CBT is an established, evidence-based treatment for adult ADHD. My CBT approach in this workbook is implementation-focused, so you can adapt the skills as you see fit to your life circumstances. If you struggle with procrastination, you can use antiprocrastination skills to get started on tasks you don't feel like doing. If you struggle with keeping track of commitments, you can draw on time-management skills, including the use of a daily planner and to-do lists. If your coping difficulties affect your work and personal relationships, antiprocrastination and time-management skills will help these, too. Additional targeted skills will help you improve your relationships and reduce your sensitivities. The CBT skills and strategies for adult ADHD draw on a range of understandings of human behavior, especially the intersection of thoughts and emotions.

The Adult ADHD and Anxiety Workbook is written for adults with ADHD whose coping difficulties are complicated by emotional overwhelm, particularly the spectrum of anxiety, worry, apprehensions, jitters, nervous discomfort, and uneasiness when facing the tasks, chores, demands, and roles of adult life. This is a fitting definition of the adult ADHD–anxiety connection.

You need not have a formal anxiety diagnosis to benefit from this book. As noted, ADHD is likely the chief source of your anxiety. You may typically describe yourself as easygoing until facing a project deadline or, worse, an I-have-to-do-it job without any deadline, requiring you to organize and execute a work plan on your own timeline without any external scaffolding. This is when stress and anxieties kick in. At first, these discomforts make you procrastinate and avoid tasks. Then you reach a point of no return when there are no other options but to do the task. Here anxiety transforms into panic, the rocket fuel to binge work on a project the night before it's due. This leads to an unhealthy, unsustainable, and stressful lifestyle.

Before reaching that point, though, otherwise reasonable task plans likely got labeled in your mind as work, chores, tedious, or boring and consequently are now exponentially more stressful and thereby susceptible to procrastination (Jaffe 2013). This connection probably stems from your lifetime struggles with ADHD, which triggers anxiety. Even if your anxiety is confined to circumscribed matters, the ideas and suggestions in this book will help you more effectively face them and free up time and peace of mind for yourself.

You may have picked up this book because you've been lugging around anxiety for a long time and have improved some but have hit a wall. This is what happens for many adults with ADHD who were diagnosed with depression or anxiety before learning they had ADHD. You may sense that there's something else causing the troubling inconsistency in your life.

Many women, like Kelly, who later identified with ADHD, first sought treatment for anxiety or depression. In fact, women with ADHD may be more prone to the adult ADHD–anxiety combination (Fuller-Thomson, Carrique, and MacNeil 2022). The prevalence of adult ADHD is about equal between men and women, but many women go undiagnosed until adulthood and on average are diagnosed later in life than men. There's still a greater ratio of boys to girls diagnosed in the school-age years. This difference is attributed to the fact that hyperactivity and its effects seen in boys are more readily identified in the classroom. Girls' inattention and distractibility in the classroom and at home often goes unnoticed.

If any of these stories resonate with you, welcome. This workbook is for you, too. Let's now turn to what the book aims to do for you and how you can make it work best for you.

How Do I Get the Most Out of the Book?

There are ample opportunities for you to personalize this book. To help you identify personally relevant examples, chapters have reflection and practice exercises related to your experience of ADHD.

There are explicit suggestions and frameworks not only for what to do (or not do) but also for how to implement the advice. Please remember that one of the insights from the contemporary view of ADHD is that it's a performance or implementation problem, not a knowledge problem. You might have the thought, *If I could do these exercises, I wouldn't need this book* or *I know exactly what to do, but I just don't do it.* Much like different routes you can take when driving to a destination, there are many ways to cope well with ADHD and regain control of your life. If any of the coping skills and tools aren't an exact fit with your style, you can adapt them to your circumstances. The coping strategies are blueprints for what to do that I hope will work for you, but focus on the skills that work best for you and customize the skills and tools. When they work for you, you'll use them more consistently and successfully.

A coping action plan that you'll encounter throughout the book has three steps, which can be abbreviated as SAP.

- Be *specific*.

- Define tasks in *actionable* steps.

- Implement at targeted *pivot points*.

Targeted pivot points are designated transition points where you can actively shape the course of your day by implementing specific, doable plans, such as coping strategies. For example, a targeted pivot point might be a set time each day, such as your morning wake time. It could also be tied to a recurring action in the flow of your day, such as after dinner.

The idea is to make valued tasks a series of doable action steps that you believe you'll do, even if you're skeptical. Your challenge is akin to someone who says they can't cook. Then they're given a series of actionable steps: Get a saucepan, fill it with water, place it on the stove, bring the water to a boil, add the spaghetti—yadda, yadda, yadda. By completing the steps, they've just cooked. With this workbook, you'll have skills to practice and hone. Thus, use the strategies outlined in this workbook, including the SAP plan described above, as recipe suggestions that you personalize to your tastes.

CBT has been proven to be effective. It's the implementation of what works that is this workbook's focal point. Much like the recipe/cooking analogy, even experienced cooks execute steps to make a dish. From this foundation, they experiment with new dishes and spruce up old ones. We're going to be making some dishes together. There'll be recipes of skills, tools, and exercises to help you meet your goals, including dealing with ADHD and its accompanying stress and anxieties. You'll practice these exercises with examples from your life. Then you'll go and use them in real time, which is like putting your dish in the oven and eventually enjoying the finished product, your positive coping results. You'll be the master chef of your adult ADHD–anxiety kitchen.

I invite you to take the first specific, actionable step by turning to chapter 1, your first pivot point. Let's get cooking!

Understanding ADHD, Anxiety, and Their Connection

When Barry completed his ADHD evaluation, he greeted news of his diagnosis by slowly bending forward. After a moment he straightened up, releasing a big exhale of relief. He now had an explanation that helped him make sense of his long-standing, confounding struggles with disorganization and keeping up with responsibilities. These happened first at college and later at work and at home, despite hearing so much about his potential and his many efforts to work harder and do better.

When Kelly completed her evaluation for ADHD, she also greeted news of her diagnosis by slowly bending forward. After a moment she straightened up, releasing a torrent of tears. After collecting herself, she described feeling equal parts relief with having a way to understand her struggle and mourning about how her life could've been different with an earlier diagnosis. A forced academic leave from college was the reason she sought the evaluation; she too had heard so much about her potential and that she only needed to work harder and apply herself better.

ADHD takes no prisoners. Many people like Barry, Kelly, Susan, and Trent and maybe you at some point lament lost jobs or promotions, relationship breakups and lost friendships, unfinished degree programs, and other lost opportunities and goals. The power of an accurate diagnosis of ADHD and how it can change your outlook is captured by the title of an early popular book on adult ADHD called *You Mean I'm Not Lazy, Stupid, or Crazy?!* (Kelly and Ramundo 1993).

It's not the diagnostic label, per se, that opens the avenue for change. It's seeing clearly how ADHD affects your day-to-day affairs—what it means for real life. When you see and understand

ADHD, rather than merely trying to gauge your attention and restlessness, you can catch ADHD in action. Better yet, you can predict and plan for navigating trouble spots. The skills and strategies in this workbook are designed to help you better organize and execute these and other intentions. What's more, they'll help you see and deal with the stress and anxiety of ADHD and how the coexisting conditions magnify and are magnified by each other. This is the essence of the change process in CBT for adult ADHD and anxiety.

So, let's focus on what you want to get out of this book and capture some of your initial thoughts. Your goals are your motivations for facing ADHD and anxiety in the first place and will be important go-to reminders for you.

Reflection

Write down your goals for using this workbook. Nothing is too big or too small, anything from finishing that last college course to folding and putting away the clean laundry. The more specific and actionable the goal, the more likely you'll do it.

_____   _____

_____   _____

_____   _____

_____   _____

_____   _____

_____   _____

_____   _____

_____   _____

Because of a lifetime of ADHD undermining your efforts, your plans and goals are colored (and not rose-colored) by your past frustrations and failures. These, in turn, become associated with feelings of anxiety and ugh. This is your anxiety signaling you that such plans and goals pose danger or at least the risk for failure, disappointment, or stress and tedium. There's a quick, enticing way to deal with this feeling to make it go away faster than any medication—avoidance. But this is precisely how anxiety creates the vicious loop of making you sidestep endeavors you know you can do but that have also been markedly frustrating for you. These experiences make it even harder to overcome these feelings and execute your intentions.

You probably picked up this book because of this vicious loop of ADHD and anxiety and its effects on your life. You might have picked it up and set it down, thinking, *I know this stuff, I know what I need to do. I don't need another book telling me these things.*

But we're jumping ahead. What is it about adult ADHD that makes your endeavors such a struggle when everyone else seems able to manage? How does anxiety get hitched to ADHD in a way that makes ADHD even tougher to deal with? The next sections will review ADHD, anxiety, and their merger to get us on the same page, setting the stage for the business of breaking the cycle and taking back your life.

What Is ADHD?

But what does adult ADHD *really* feel and look like? Most certainly attention and hyperactivity (and impulsivity) are ADHD's defining symptom clusters. They're not bad or wrong descriptors, but they're incomplete. When you scanned this book and thought it might be helpful, you probably didn't think, *Oh, this will help my attention, hyperactivity, and impulsivity.*

The introduction presented the contemporary view of ADHD as a chronic self-regulation inefficiency and inconsistency. More specifically, it's difficulties with the various building blocks of self-regulation, the executive functions. Here's a list of categories from executive-function rating scales.

- **Time management:** the organization of behavior over time, working toward goals

- **Planning and organizing time and tasks and using available resources, such as instructions:** keeping track of commitments and stuff, using help

- **Impulse control or self-inhibition:** resisting temptation, delayed gratification

- **Emotional self-regulation:** gearing up to do something, soothing your feelings and reactions, or both

- **Motivation:** an ability to feel like doing a hard thing when it is the right thing to do

- **Memory/working memory:** recalling information, keeping plans in mind, or both

- **Action:** physical or mental restlessness, directing your behavior

- **Focus/attention:** ability to attend to what is important and avoid distractions

- **Effort:** devoting necessary time and energy to a task, often over multiple work sessions

- **Flexibility:** ability to adapt to circumstances, cognitively and emotionally

- **Getting started on things:** initiating action and effort

- **Self-monitoring:** checking in with how you are doing and tracking what you are doing

- **Organizing materials:** managing stuff

- **Shifting between tasks:** juggling different roles and responsibilities

- **Problem-solving:** developing and implementing solutions and decisions

Reflection

Let's look at your executive-function profile. Using the same list from above, consider each category as it applies to you. If something struck you about a category—for example, it's a challenge for you—make a note to capture your initial thoughts.

Time management

_____

_____

Planning and organizing time and
tasks and using available
resources, such as instructions

_____

_____

Impulse control or self-inhibition

_____

_____

Emotional self-regulation

_____

_____

Motivation

_____

_____

Memory/working memory

_____

_____

Action

_____

_____

Focus/attention

_____

_____

Effort

_____

_____

Flexibility

_____

_____

Getting started on things

_____

_____

Self-monitoring

_____

_____

Organizing materials

_____

_____

Shifting between tasks

_____

_____

Problem-solving

_____

_____

This list lays bare how executive-function difficulties and the consistent inconsistency of ADHD create stress and worry when you face multiple adult role expectations. This illustrates the adult ADHD–anxiety connection in action. In this way, ADHD can feel like food poisoning. Not the literal physical effects of eating tainted food, mind you. Rather, ADHD taints and punctuates the plans, goals, and endeavors you are invested in, motivated to work on, and really want to accomplish. These include both have-to and want-to endeavors. Your experiences of ADHD and ongoing coping difficulties can make them exercises in stress that leave you frustrated and feeling worse about yourself, like that sushi you typically enjoy leaving you doubled over with stomach cramps. Consequently, the next time you think about ordering sushi, even if you logically know this time it'll be fine, nausea kicks in to warn and protect you, which is analogous to anxiety being the emotional nausea that kicks in with ADHD, reminding and warning you of past frustrations.

What ADHD looks like is the image of an ADHD GPS in which you enter your day's plans as destinations. You then track how closely you follow your designated routes and whether you reach your destinations, that is, fulfill your plans. Did you take detours but still arrive where you wanted as planned? Or did you change directions before realizing that even if you turned back now, you wouldn't reach your destination in time? Extending the analogy, while going in the wrong direction, you might have run out of gas, had a car breakdown, or faced other stress that undid you getting to your itinerary. Perhaps negative consequences extended beyond those for today's trip. Maybe, being late meant that you've missed out on an opportunity. This mythical ADHD GPS also tracks your attention because although you're facing your office computer, presumably working, your brain and attention are stuck in park, watching silly pet videos, idling but still burning fuel.

These are all analogies for executive-function problems commonly faced by adults with ADHD. CBT can be particularly helpful in working with adult ADHD because it focuses on the implementation of skills and strategies to help you follow through on your priorities and work around your executive-function weaknesses to avoid such problems.

===================== Reflection =====================

Below are some examples of common executive-function problems that are sources of stress and anxiety for many adults with ADHD. For those that apply to you, rate how much of a problem they pose to you and write down your answer next to the item. Use a 1-to-5 rating scale with 1 = not a problem; 2 = occasionally, sometimes; 3 = often; 4 = very often; 5 = regularly (daily). There's no total score or formal profile. Simply see what your ratings reveal as areas of focus.

_____   Lateness or worries about being late for work, school, or social meetings

_____   Lateness or worries about being late for scheduled medical appointments

_____   Losing track of and misjudging time and tasks, that is, how long things take

_____   Difficulties keeping track of commitments and deadlines

_____   Difficulties sticking to plans

_____   Difficulties getting started on tasks

_____   Difficulties returning to ongoing tasks and projects

_____   Difficulties keeping up with chores and administrative tasks at home

_____   Feeling stressed and overwhelmed with plans and commitments

_____   Difficulties initiating contact with people, such as home-repair people or business associates

_____   Difficulties returning phone calls, texts, emails, or other communications

_____   Difficulties breaking down plans into steps and doing the steps

_____   Resistance to making plans and commitments

_____   Delays due to perfectionism

_____   Difficulties handling feedback or criticism from others

_____   Using coping strategies for a while but then giving up on them

That's a long list! Remember the comparably long list of executive-function categories earlier in the chapter? Your executive functions play a role in virtually everything you do. Your self-control uses up a lot of energy, too. Such matters are particularly exhausting for adults with ADHD. This is consistent with recent findings of higher rates of fatigue among adults with ADHD (Guntuku et al. 2019; Rogers et al. 2017; Young 2013).

The human brain is about 2 percent of the body's mass, but it spends 20 percent of the body's calorie budget (Levitin 2014). This energy goes into actions such as:

- **Impulse control:** This includes resisting temptations.

- **Thinking and planning:** Did you ever say to yourself, *It makes me tired just thinking about this?*

- **Making choices and decisions:** This is known as *choice* or *decision fatigue.*

- **Task-switching:** There's no multitasking—every switch is a brain drain!

- **Other sorts of mental work:** This includes reading this book and being on in social settings.

The level of mental demand of different tasks is called *cognitive load,* which creates physical fatigue because the mental is physical. For example, daydreaming uses eleven calories per hour, reading forty-two, and sitting in a class burns sixty-five calories per hour when learning new information (Levitin 2014). Other things like poor sleep, illness, or stress can deplete your self-control battery, too. This is a reason that I will emphasize self-care and self-compassion (see chapter 8) as important tasks to help you replenish your energy and your overall well-being.

It's time to circle back to the question of what ADHD is and the relevance of the answer to this book.

First, the various problems that led you to seek out this book are rooted in executive-function difficulties that underlie ADHD. The operative mission of executive functions boils down to "the efficiency with which you do what you set out to do" (Goldstein and Naglieri 2014). Even seemingly straightforward goals, like working on a report, require initiation and execution of the necessary steps to accomplish the goal. This is the work of your executive functions, such as initiating and persisting on a task, dealing with people, avoiding distractions but still taking breaks as needed, and transitioning between different duties and roles.

Second, the consistent inconsistency of ADHD is due to the fact your executive-functioning baseline is a moving target. ADHD is characterized by chronic, persistent difficulties and unpredictability in organization and follow-through. Accordingly, your functioning can be extremely up or down, depending on what you're facing that requires organization and follow-through. Colleague and

ADHD expert Thomas Brown calls this the fundamental paradox of ADHD. In some settings you can do quite well, if not exceptionally. In others, you run the risk of considerable struggles and frustrations. Your performance may vary wildly from one day to the next without apparent reason, an inconsistency that is supremely unsettling and, guess what, quite anxiety-provoking and disruptive to plans.

Last, it's important to remember that ADHD is not a knowledge problem but a performance problem when it comes to coping (Ramsay and Rostain 2016). Your frustrations and ugh feelings originate from the disconnect of your know-how and your demonstrated capabilities (*I've done this before and done it well*) on the one side. On the other side are the radical ups and downs in execution (*I know that I can do it. I don't trust I will do it when I plan to or must do it*).

Reflection

Let's take another reflection moment for your workbook goals. On the lines below, list some example activities in your daily life that you know you can do. Include some things that you can do well and that you'd like to do more consistently. For example, are you good at starting your day, or do you end up running late? Do you have a plan for the flow of your day that works, or do you have a hard time keeping to it? Do you have some good habits, such as completing a certain household chore or exercising regularly, that are strengths you can build on?

With the focus on all the problems that come with ADHD, you might be thinking, *And this book is supposed to make me feel better how?* Sorry for the downers, but ADHD can really wear down your confidence, self-esteem, and sense of efficacy. Thus, recognizing the effects of ADHD is a first step in this process.

You might be feeling a little stressed and anxious about the prospect of change at this point. It's no surprise that anxiety is the most common emotional theme experienced by adults with ADHD. Living with ADHD for so long has made you prone to feeling anxiety when facing tasks and goals. In fact, sometimes a little bit of anxiety is useful to signal that you're doing exactly what you should be doing, like an athlete before a competition or you before doing workbook exercises. The next section provides an overview of this relationship with anxiety.

What Is Anxiety?

Anxiety is a future-oriented, gut-level emotional and mental apprehension about vague, very unlikely yet plausible, nonzero risks, often framed as what-if scenarios (Leahy 2005). You might experience this in anticipation of working on something that you know is difficult for you, like personal finances.

Anxiety is an emotional state, often experienced as negative insofar as it is marked by a degree of unease and discomfort, and sometimes agitation. You feel it when you're nervous, apprehensive, or downright scared. I'll use the word *unpleasant* versus *negative* because the capacity to feel anxiety is beneficial. It's like how the feeling of pain signals that you've sustained sunburn so you can treat it. Anxiety helps you judge potential dangers and risks, such as when nearing an unchained, snarling dog. On the other hand, adaptive, low-level stress is a motivator, spurring you to prepare before a work presentation, leave early for an appointment to beat traffic, or schedule a preventative medical screening. Each of these tasks fosters your overall well-being and, in turn, reduces overall stress.

What are your tells for anxiety? What feelings and sensations do you have, and what words do you use to describe them? Where do you feel it in your body? In what circumstances do you often notice worry, anxiety, stress, or other unsettling feelings?

Your emotions are guided by your personal experiences, what you've learned about your world. Your brain and emotions make predictions about situations you encounter by drawing on what's happened in comparable conditions before. These predictions are also shaped by your here-and-now reading of what's going on around you relative to your current intentions.

This is the way in which ADHD forms a relationship with anxiety. Your life history with the inherent unpredictability of ADHD makes many of your tasks, endeavors, and roles fraught with a layer of uncertainty, even risk. It's probably not life-or-death risk or even risk of physical harm, like facing the snarling dog. It's Barry's uncertainty about carrying out his work plan due to the discomfort and tedium he anticipates stomaching. His reaction was steeped in his frustrations with innumerable school assignments and other writing duties, even as seemingly clear-cut as email responses. His anxieties also recalled all the disappointing grades on those school assignments despite the hours he spent on them, troubles with previous monthly reports, and a chorus of voices reminding him of the potential he could reach if he only worked harder. These memories informed his anticipations about writing tasks that over time were infused with worry feelings. Even the idea of facing the monthly report triggered his ugh reaction in nanoseconds. Barry's reaction makes perfect sense based on his past but was not aligned with his current goal to complete his work plan.

As with other emotions, anxiety's signals require some deciphering. This includes considering your current situation, history, and objectives to determine how you can best interpret and handle them relative to your intentions. ADHD adds a layer to this process because, as with Barry, it affects all the factors informing and guiding your anticipations and reflexive interpretations, which anxiety uses to spot risks.

For example, Trent is a friendly person, but his distractibility and forgetfulness caused problems for him in all sorts of social situations when he was younger. He forgot promises, dinner reservations, and band practices. These ADHD-related snafus, types of things that still happened in adulthood, turned his anxiety into an overactive alarm for disappointment and rejection. As a result, he slowly withdrew from all but an innermost circle of safe people. He didn't trust himself to make a good impression, so he adopted a deferential stance to try to avoid disapproval. Thus, his anxiety goaded him to play it safe and dismiss friendly overtures from others to connect as too risky. This response deprived him of potential friends.

Reflection

Think about whether you face any commonplace situations where ADHD creates anxiety for you and interferes with your intentions. Write down your thoughts.

_____

_____

_____

_____

_____

Why Does ADHD Make Me So Stressed and Anxious?

Let's take a closer look at the adult ADHD–anxiety connection. One frustration of the consistent inconsistency of ADHD is that when dealing with matters that you enjoy, find interesting, or are confident you can accomplish, you may be anxiety-free. You're a great consultant face-to-face but agonize over the summary report, for instance. You earned As in challenging, interesting classes, but you fell behind and had to drop easy but boring courses. You're never late for personal training sessions but forget meetings with your child's teacher. When facing situations that expose your ADHD-related weaknesses, you may be likely to seize up with emotions such as anxiety, fear, worry, or stress because your history shows that they're risky for you.

An aspect of changing your relationship with anxiety (and other emotions) as part of coping with ADHD is to decipher the themes of their signals to you. Until recently, the theme associated with anxiety was the perception of threat or danger risks. No doubt, these are still relevant. We use a lot of words interchangeably to describe anxiety, but let's differentiate it from the more common ones, which include fear, worry, and stress.

Fear is a current, visceral feeling when facing (or misperceiving) an immediate danger, such as seeing a spider (or reacting to a rubber toy spider that you thought was real), a near-accident while driving, or other here-and-now events. In contrast, anxiety is future oriented.

Worry, also deemed "death by doubt" (Hallowell 1997), is rumination about specific, real-life events, such as taking a high-stakes exam or running late for a job interview. For example, you may worry about an email, stew over it to make sure your thoughts are organized, and end up spending an hour on a twenty-word message.

Stress is a feeling that runs through anxiety. Stress is your reaction to an external demand, such as being overextended at work and then having to deal with a car problem, too. Even positive demands are stressful, such as receiving a job promotion or readying for a vacation. You probably use the word *stress* for the feeling of juggling all your duties and responsibilities. You'll hear friends complain about similar life stresses. ADHD adds degrees of difficulty due to executive dysfunction. For example, you may work to employ all the necessary organization and time-management skills to juggle work and family commitments but still fall behind. The differences in the degree of stress are like two people describing heavy winds. The person without ADHD is concerned that a stiff breeze will carry away loose papers. Someone with ADHD worries about hurricane-force winds blowing the roof off their house. Generally, the adult ADHD–anxiety connection stems from the apprehensive associations with various tasks based on past ADHD-related frustrations.

The adult ADHD–anxiety connection doesn't have to match a formal anxiety diagnostic category, such as a phobia, to cause problems and be worthy of attention. The most relevant anxiety issue for the adult ADHD–anxiety connection is that of generalized anxiety disorder (GAD), which affects 2 to 6 percent of the general population (Brown, O'Leary, and Barlow 2001; Roemer, Eustis, and Orsillo 2021). GAD has been called the *basic* anxiety, akin to an anxious disposition, like excessively stressing about unfounded risks for identity theft. I'd make the case that the worries associated with dealing with ADHD are come by honestly. These feelings are the effects of long-standing ADHD-related frustrations despite your best efforts to power through them. GAD is a good catchall for the adult ADHD–anxiety the next section discusses.

How Did ADHD and Anxiety Get Connected in My Life?

A study cited in the book's introduction, which found that women are more prone to the adult ADHD–anxiety connection, also found a strong association of ADHD and GAD in a national sample of Canadian adults (Fuller-Thomson, Carrique, and MacNeil 2022). In this study, more than 10 percent of adults with GAD also reported a diagnosis of ADHD. Adults with ADHD were twice as likely to report GAD than individuals without ADHD. This really wasn't shocking news, as the adult ADHD–anxiety connection had been previously well established (Barkley 2015; Children and Adults with Attention-Deficit/Hyperactivity Disorder [CHADD] 2015; Chung et al. 2019).

Feelings of Stress

A feature of the GAD diagnosis directly relevant for ADHD is that of worry or apprehension, which is often described by people as feeling stressed. The following physical symptoms of GAD partially overlap with ADHD:

- restlessness, which includes fidgetiness or an urge to always be doing something, or pacing when worried

- concentration difficulties or poor sustained focus on tasks or in meetings or conversations, including due to worrisome thoughts

- sleep problems, most often problems falling or staying asleep, or problems turning off your mind, especially from ruminative worry

You might notice other mixed anxiety and stress reactions, too, like headaches, muscle tension, or high blood pressure. Overlapping symptoms can magnify other health conditions like irritable bowel syndrome.

Living with ADHD is stressful. We saw how anxiety for Barry, Kelly, Susan, and Trent was rooted in their experiences, especially before learning they had ADHD. Similar reactions you experience make sense because anxiety and worry are feelings based on your right-now perceptions of what's happening, informed by your past. These perceptions help you determine how to stay on track for your objectives. For adults with ADHD, making plans in the first place means facing and dealing with the future and what-if anxiety. Hence, the consistent inconsistency of ADHD adds a degree of uncertainty to plans. The thought of setting up a schedule triggers stress and resistance for many adults with ADHD. This is due to the real possibility that they might not do what they set out to do, activating another layer of worry about yet another possible failure—but, then again, maybe not.

Dealing with this uncertainty is an important element when addressing generalized anxiety (Dugas et al. 1998) and especially when living with ADHD. ADHD introduces a huge what-if whenever considering your objectives and plans.

Feelings of Uncertainty

When you feel stressed about catching up at work or anticipating an upcoming performance review, do you ever try to talk yourself through it? For example, you could remind yourself that the work might not take that long or list reasons why your boss's ratings will be okay. What happens then? Are you comforted and at ease? Or do you think of what-if scenarios, like *What if my work takes a lot longer than I expect?* or *What if my boss is fed up with my lateness and puts me on a performance improvement plan? That's the first step in getting fired!* Do you keep grinding on these worst-case scenarios to the point you're too stressed to work or you toss and turn all night before your review?

These are examples of how *uncertainty* and, more specifically, *intolerance of uncertainty*—wrestling with the unresolvable nonzero risk in life—stoke anxiety and symptoms like uneasiness, sleep difficulties, and stress (Dugas et al. 1998). If you have trouble handling situations and choices that are not 100 percent clear, you may also question your opinions and decisions and feel paralyzed by doubt. You might have problems dealing with the stress of unanticipated changes such that you abandon plans altogether rather than persist when they change, for example, by rescheduling a missed appointment. You might notice that changing plans bothers you more than other people.

Compare intolerance of uncertainty with the descriptions of adult ADHD and executive dysfunction. As I said previously, ADHD is characterized as consistent inconsistency with organization and follow-through on valued goals and endeavors (both have-to's and the want-to's) and difficulties with activities such as chores at home, work projects, social events, and hobbies. Effectively managing adult responsibilities and objectives, like keeping up with chores, work, exercise, parenting, and all the rest, requires sustained effort and trust in your abilities to follow through and deal with uncertainty. You must especially stay on track to achieve longer-range goals. It is when managing these responsibilities and accompanying uncertainties that ADHD and anxiety conspire to create problems.

Reflection

Think about both the intolerance of uncertainty as seen in anxiety and the uncertainty or unpredictability introduced into your life by ADHD. What examples resonate for you and your experiences?

_____

_____

_____

_____

_____

_____

_____

As one client said to me after I described ADHD as difficulties organizing behavior across time: "That's it! My boss always says if he needs something from me in ten minutes, I deliver it in five. If I have two weeks, it takes me a month." When something is needed right now, you may feel clear, focused, and able to respond immediately, like you would if you were defusing a bomb. Having two weeks, though, provides a lot of leeway. The project must be done, but not right now. The finish line is way out there, which opens a rabbit hole. The takeaway is that ADHD itself is an uncertainty generator.

The adult ADHD–anxiety connection helps make sense of and illustrates how difficulties and frustrations from ADHD are connected to and super sized by anxiety. The next section will circle back on the inconsistency in the adult ADHD–anxiety connection to pinpoint another vital ingredient that this workbook will target—avoidance.

The Inconsistency of ADHD

Preliminary evidence supports the role of intolerance of uncertainty in the adult ADHD–anxiety connection (Lokuge et al. 2023). ADHD creates uncertainties in your life. You've lived them. ADHD is an uncertainty generator and an inconsistency generator. As many clients have told me: "I know what I need to do. I know I can do it. But I don't trust myself to do it when I must do it." This self-mistrust (Ramsay 2020) stems from innumerable frustrations, letdowns, and failures, despite best efforts—working twice as hard for half as much, as a colleague once described the plight of adults with ADHD. What's more, such frustrations are not isolated events, onetime hiccups that you merely brush off. Instead, the effects of ADHD continually punctuate your efforts and strengths, not every time but enough to keep you on edge. Whenever ADHD disrupts a plan, it's another gut punch that leaves you thinking, *Here I go again.*

You will procrastinate and forget things. The relapse rate is 100 percent. The question is how you'll manage when it happens.

This workbook will provide you with strategies and skills to help you cope better and reduce your stress and anxiety. Using them to better organize, manage, and engage with situations and your intentions will increase your success rate. In a broader sense, you'll strengthen your ability to persist through stress and uncertainty, use skills to realize your goals, and build your agency, self-efficacy, and self-trust.

Let's set the record straight about a potential misunderstanding. The implementation focus—facing and finishing what you set out to do—will be central to forthcoming chapters. This approach is *not* rooted in the conviction that you should be an automaton, always coloring inside the lines. Indeed, one of the insidious features of ADHD is that it interferes with your agency, efficacy, and accomplishment of goals. The purpose of these strategies and skills is to help you build and sustain your identity, self-expression, and well-being.

What's more, ADHD and executive functioning are not all-or-nothing propositions. You are likely able to function quite well in some settings. Now and then, you'll likely have out-of-the-blue, super-productive, focused days. Other times, though, your plans and efforts will end up being a dumpster fire of struggles and disappointment. As real and valid as the positive days and your talents are, you may still hear refrains, like "You did fine yesterday, why can't you do it today?" or "You see, you can do it. You choose not to do it." You might even say these things to yourself. It may feel as though your skills and strengths are held against you and end up as criticisms.

Reflection

Before moving on, I invite you to reflect on situations where you notice the things that you do well but ADHD interferes with. These might be things that others compliment you on, but you think, *If only they knew how disorganized I am.* You may feel like an imposter.

_____   _____

_____   _____

_____   _____

_____   _____

_____   _____

_____   _____

_____   _____

_____   _____

The problem with the inconsistency of ADHD and anxiety is that the dumpster-fire days become associated with difficulties, poor results, criticisms, and other burns. No surprise, then, that such endeavors, in turn, trigger apprehension and the ugh feeling the next time you face them. This is your anxiety signaling for self-protection. Left unchecked, your ADHD-related anxiety activates escape-avoidance despite your best intentions. Let's look at this situation in more detail.

Avoidance

Avoidance is a common reaction to situations that trigger anxiety and is the primary response among adults with ADHD (Bodalski, Knouse, and Kovalev 2019). However, it's mostly a maladaptive response that binds ADHD and anxiety. There are many healthy examples of escape-avoidance, such as adhering to hurricane evacuation warnings. We're focusing on unhelpful or maladaptive escape-avoidance. For example, you've probably faced times when you knew you were procrastinating but did it anyway. Later, when facing the stress and other effects of your procrastination, you likely berated yourself, asking, *Why do I always do this?*

Here's why. The immediate, physical relief of removing or avoiding something anxiety-provoking—even if your logical brain knows you'll pay a price later—is a hard-to-resist impulse. Avoidance provides relief the nanosecond you decide to escape-avoid, and the relief (ahhh) feels good, at least for now. You still must face the problem or task later, but you've given yourself a reprieve. This maladaptive pattern, based on the removal of discomfort from perceived risk or danger, is the classic recipe for avoidance in cases of anxiety (Rosqvist 2005). It's also why your ability to tolerate discomfort and ugh feelings is often the most essential emotional coping skill for managing the adult ADHD–anxiety connection (Ramsay 2020).

The avoidance described above illustrates the effects of negative reinforcement. *Negative reinforcement* is the removal of something aversive or bothersome, which increases the likelihood you'll do that behavior again. Using an umbrella on a rainy day to avoid getting wet is an example of beneficial negative reinforcement. The emotional reprieve you experience due to the escape-avoidance of the discomfort of facing tedious tasks, on the other hand, negatively reinforces and thus strengthens the maladaptive pattern and increases the likelihood of more procrastination and avoidance. In contrast, *positive reinforcement* is an incentive that increases the likelihood that you'll repeat a behavior—you wake up early to get to the bakery when it opens to get your favorite pastry before it sells out. (Note that negative reinforcement is not punishment. *Punishment* is a consequence that is designed to reduce a behavior, such as a speeding ticket.)

When you eventually get around to carrying out a task you've avoided, such as Barry with his work report, you might think, *That wasn't that bad. Why did I wait so long?* Other times, you'll suffer what is known as the *ADHD tax*, the financial costs of procrastination, such as a credit card late fee. Matters such as being late with a work project have extended effects on how your supervisor views your performance. Your report might be great, but you lose status points with your boss for lateness. But such delayed outcomes are typically not compelling enough to override here-and-now escape-avoidance for adults with ADHD. This is why time time-management and antiprocrastination skills covered in chapters 4 and 5 are so necessary.

If uncertainty connects ADHD and anxiety, escape-avoidance cements them. You're often the only one witnessing the extra time and effort and other costs of your procrastination, such as a late-night stint working on a report or a credit card late fee. Often enough, though, others are affected, such as when your child misses a field trip because you didn't sign the permission form, or your work team's schedule is delayed because you delivered your part late. The time, effort, and energy devoted to repeatedly putting a task off, while still holding it in mind, until you eventually get it done under pressure are tedious and exhausting. The cognitive load of not doing drains you. What's more, it siphons time and energy from self-care and other things you'd rather do.

In fact, escape-avoidance is considered the top issue for adults with ADHD (Bodalski, Knouse, and Kovalev 2019). Let's look at more examples of avoidance and its relation to the adult ADHD–anxiety connection.

What Does the Adult ADHD–Anxiety Connection Look and Feel Like?

The form of anxiety usually described by adults with ADHD is not like those, say, of classic panic attacks. When you're facing various necessary but uninteresting tasks, you're more likely to describe sinking feelings that signal anxiety, such as mild dread, apprehension, and anticipation of tedium. All of these are variations of discomfort and ugh feelings. The anxiety experienced with ADHD might be sprinkled with doses of *disgust,* a feeling of repulsion tied to a task, like in the example that ADHD feels like food poisoning. Recognizing, normalizing, and managing these layers of discomfort is an emotional skill this workbook will help you practice.

Following are descriptions from adults with ADHD of different manifestations of the adult ADHD–anxiety connection. These examples may help you recognize your own anxiety reactions.

Overwhelm Anxiety

Although the word *overwhelm* is ordinarily used to describe the magnitude of an emotion, such as overwhelming guilt, many adults with ADHD I've seen use the term to describe their abiding apprehension, as in "I feel a sense of overwhelm." *Overwhelm anxiety* seems to capture feelings associated with facing a looming cloud of have-to and want-to tasks and obligations. Yes, each task comes with its own worry and uncertainty, but the whole feels more daunting than the sum of its parts.

You've probably gotten the advice to break down large tasks into smaller steps, called *chunking.* It's good advice. The technical term is *event segmentation* followed by the *sequencing* of steps, which are duties of the executive functions (Levitin 2014). But when you think about chunking and sequencing, I'm guessing that you often feel swamped and frozen at the prospect of facing all you must do and sidestep it. This is the very sort of pivot point where you can employ your workbook skills to deal with issues like procrastination more effectively.

Performance/Implementation Anxiety

Even when you generate an ADHD-friendly to-do list, mild apprehension is enough to nudge you into doing something else, anything else, to avoid doing what's on the list. This is especially true when the to-do items, like "organize office," are too broad, vague, and nonspecific. You know you're capable of the job. Worded as such, though, it looks (and thereby feels) daunting. It's no wonder that you're tempted to do something else instead. As odd as it sounds, you might suddenly be motivated to do chores, like unloading the dishwasher, to reassure yourself you're being productive. Of course, you're really choosing to do something you see as more doable to avoid the perceived stress of your plan to organize the office. In this workbook, you'll learn ways to repurpose the characteristics of the escape task, like emptying the dishwasher, to follow through on your priority task and overcome performance/implementation anxiety.

Planning Anxiety

The avoidance of making plans in the first place is a preemptive strike to dodge ADHD-related performance anxiety. Having plans or expectations may activate stress and doubts about your ability to implement them. This can be an aspect of overwhelm anxiety, so you avoid making plans altogether. *Planning anxiety* and consequent avoidance via other tasks results in feeling busy, which soothes stress in the near-term, but makes you feel like you're falling behind and unproductive in the long-term.

You might say, "I work better without restrictions." That's fine if it works. However, without plans, you settle for tasks with smaller-sooner rewards and never get around to tasks with larger-later payoffs. For example, you catch up on errands, but don't start your work project or set up your easel to paint. Part of you wants to finish the report or paint, but planning these activities is more stressful in the near term and likely includes worries that your report or painting will be lacking.

Forgetting-to-Remember Anxiety

Forgetting-to-remember anxiety manifests as getting stuck on something you don't want to forget. By repeatedly hitting your mental refresh button, you keep it in the forefront of your mind. Unfortunately, this refreshing uses up mental space and energy, known as cognitive load, which saps attention and energy for other tasks, including quieting your mind for sleep (Levitin 2014).

A second manifestation of this anxiety is uneasiness with the idea that you might have missed or forgotten something important—even though there is no evidence that you have. A student may feel caught up on homework only to receive an incomplete grade due to an assignment they overlooked. Maybe you've gotten a notice that you missed an appointment that you only then recalled. Often this free-floating, forgetting-to-remember anxiety will bother you even when you are on top of things. Even the satisfying feeling of being on top of things is tied to past examples when you felt that way and were wrong. *Externalization of information,* a fancy way of saying write down plans or other things you want to remember, helps free up mental space and energy and promotes implementation. In the case of a planner system, which we'll cover, it also gives you a record of what you've done. This is a nice way to document your accomplishments.

Social Rejection Anxiety

The *social rejection anxiety* experienced with ADHD is not the same as social anxiety disorder. Instead, it's like Trent's bracing or being on guard for others' disapproval and criticisms. Even if these don't occur, many adults with ADHD are sensitive to missteps with others, such as saying the wrong thing, lateness, or a perceived loss of standing with others, which is a core human worry (Wright 1994). However, like most things, this worry is especially cutting for adults with ADHD (Beaton, Sirois, and Milne 2020).

Some of your frustrations with ADHD may occur privately, such as calling in sick to finish the report you started too late. Often, though, others witness your ADHD-related slipups or are affected by them, such as your misplaced car keys making you late to meet your spouse. Others in your life probably give you unsolicited coping advice or commentary that only aggravates your frustration. Such repeated difficulties in essential matters can erode relationships, leading to breakups or passive rejection by friends, who gradually stop reaching out or responding to your messages. You might face criticisms or hurtful teasing. You might feel that your struggles are dismissed, unseen, or misconstrued as showing you don't care, when that is not the case.

Reflection

Do any of the above types of anxiety resonate for you? Do you have any other anxiety types to add? Describe any specific tasks, duties, or roles and relationships that trigger your anxiety or ugh feelings.

_____

_____

_____

_____

_____

_____

_____

_____

_____

_____

Summary

This is a lot to take in. To simplify and summarize the adult ADHD–anxiety framework, the different forms of anxiety are bundled together as the discomfort or risk signals you feel when dealing with the uncertainty of ADHD. A benefit of CBT for adult ADHD is that its flexibility allows it to be adapted to your needs in terms of the implementation of executive-function coping strategies. A bonus is that this implementation-focus CBT blends strategies for treating anxiety (Rosqvist 2005).

Exposure treatment, one such strategy, is essentially confronting fears in a step-by-step manner. Each step is designed to unlearn an anxiety response and build up your ability to face typically avoided situations. The goal is to be less activated, yes, but also to accept discomfort and not be undone by anxiety. Your learning history from living with ADHD, on the other hand, has been colored by executive-function difficulties, such as poor time management, procrastination, and disorganization. Anxiety latched onto these difficulties plays a role, too.

The central focus on coping with ADHD in this workbook targets implementation of intentions. This requires engagement and exposure to things you would typically avoid or at least put off. Hence, by practicing better time-management and antiprocrastination skills in relation to your life and goals using CBT, you should also expect decreased anxiety or at least better acceptance of it. In fact, many adults with ADHD and anxiety who are prescribed a medication for ADHD report that once they're managing better, their anxiety improves without needing anxiety medication. It was ADHD causing the anxiety.

Now we're wading into the topic of what to do about the adult ADHD–anxiety connection. The next chapter will provide a framework for managing the effects of this connection using CBT for adult ADHD.

CHAPTER 2

How Cognitive Behavioral Therapy Principles Can Help

I know what I need to do. I just don't do it.

I'm great at making plans, but I don't follow them.

I'll use a planner for a while but then stop.

I get started on projects. I don't finish them.

I want to do certain things, but I get overwhelmed and end up not doing them.

Other people are fed up with me and my disorganization.

Do any of these statements sound familiar? These are some of the most common frustrations I hear from adults who are seeking help to manage their ADHD. Like you, they're motivated to make changes but have a hard time making them stick.

In this chapter, we'll discuss CBT-based strategies to address these recurring exasperations and the barriers to follow-through due to ADHD.

What Is CBT, and How Can It Help Me?

Cognitive behavioral therapy (CBT) is a form of psychotherapy that came on the scene as a therapy for depression (A. T. Beck 1967) but soon became a go-to treatment for anxiety (Beck, Emery, and Greenberg 1985). CBT emphasizes the influential role of thoughts, beliefs, and other cognitions and recognizes how examining and changing thoughts can help change feelings, behaviors, and outlooks that we use to make sense of our experiences. It's particularly helpful to people dealing with depression and anxiety.

CBT helps you understand your emotional reactions, especially when your anxiety warning signals are out of proportion to the current situation. Have you ever had an *ugh* reaction to a work project that ended in procrastination? Have you felt the stress of facing a jam-packed day of commitments only to do other things and neglect these priorities? Did you then feel more behind and stressed than when you started the day? These anxiety reactions that stem from your reflexive interpretations of what you anticipated facing are called *automatic thoughts about the situation*. Your ugh feeling might have been prompted by the thought *I must be in the mood for my work project*, with the unspoken conditional thought *If I'm not in the mood, I'm justified in putting off the task until I am*. Put this way, it seems so simple: change your thoughts and get things done. It takes practice, though, to catch and see the influence of your thoughts, and even more effort to form new outlooks.

CBT Addresses Unhelpful Thoughts

A tenet of CBT is that automatic thoughts are vulnerable to distortion. Such cognitive distortions are not delusions but simply unhelpful impressions of situations. They are unhelpful thoughts. Most adults with ADHD deal with some degree of these habitual negative expectations and self-views based on a history of ADHD frustrations. For example, the thought that you must be in the mood for a task is an all-or-nothing thought about what your emotional state should be before starting any task. However, it's possible to consider plausible alternatives, such as *No one feels like doing work. I'll start, get into it, and soon feel better.*

The cognitive distortion bias in anxiety is the exaggeration of the risk that something bad will happen, like the negative prediction that you can't face a busy day. You end up doing other, less stressful busywork. You don't make any headway on your priorities, which only heightens your stress later. The cognitive therapy component of CBT targets such unhelpful thoughts and helps you develop more helpful mindsets.

Cognitive modification skills you'll practice later involve catching and assessing your thoughts to make sure you are making fully informed judgements about situations and your options. Cognitive flexibility empowers you to take proactive coping steps and more effectively wield your agency to turn your intentions into actions. For example, when facing the stress of a busy day, you can prepare and define specific action plans for specific tasks and set realistic expectations for yourself. This includes recognizing that you might not get to everything in one day but can still have a productive day.

Ultimately, exposing yourself to stress and anxieties will help you manage them better. Cognitive change involves being willing to test and modify your thoughts. For example, you can make a realistic plan for your day and evaluate how it works out—and then repeat the process multiple times. In effect, with exposure, you'll grow bored of anxiety by facing a situation over and over until you see the bad stuff doesn't happen or your worry is worse than any difficulties you face. It's like seeing a scary movie so many times that it's no longer as scary as the first viewing (Leahy 2005). Getting practice organizing and executing your day armed with realistic expectations helps produce more positive outcomes and less stress. You'll see that you get more done on some days than others. Each is still productive, though, representing a degree of consistency, which is progress. Such behavioral outcomes help change thoughts, too.

Let's look at how CBT skills can help you accomplish this.

How Can CBT Help Me Cope Better?

Let's be clear: you could never think yourself into ADHD. Even though CBT emphasizes the influential role of cognitions, including their role in adult ADHD, it doesn't mean that thoughts cause everything.

The CBT conceptualization of adult ADHD starts with the premise that growing up with ADHD affects your life experiences from an early age. If you've been diagnosed with ADHD, you experience some degree of difficulty in adult life. You face more stress and disorganization juggling your obligations than people without ADHD. You have more unease and less time for yourself. In more extreme circumstances, you may have lost jobs, dropped out of school, had relationship turmoil, or faced money problems due to inconsistent follow-through.

All these factors affect how you make sense of yourself, your circumstances, and your future in the form of your thoughts, attitudes, and beliefs. These cognitions shape your perceived options and actions. Due to your lifelong, ADHD-driven problems and living with consistent inconsistency in various roles and relationships, you have a reflexive penchant for anxiety and disengagement, procrastination, and all forms of avoidance as default coping reactions. You're likely to end up frustrated and abandon plans due to poor, or at least inconsistent, follow-through. This leaves you gun-shy for resuming them or following new goals and dreams (Ramsay 2020; Ramsay and Rostain 2015a; 2015b; 2016).

This is how anxiety and escape-avoidance contaminate your intentions in a vicious cycle. You're going to learn ways to break this cycle. The skills and strategies in this workbook are designed to help you implement effective coping strategies for managing ADHD. You will build trust in your follow-through by facing and reducing stress and anxiety instead defaulting to escape-avoidance.

To explore how CBT works, we'll look at five different coping skill domains within CBT (Ramsay 2020):

- cognitive

- behavior

- emotion

- implementation

- interpersonal

The skills overlap and work together to help you cope better. For example, thinking differently about how you approach a stressful day will help you experiment with a plan to get a little done each day. Implementing the plan will enable you to feel less stressed and more confident in what you can handle. These categories also provide a menu of coping skills that you can use. If one skill is not working today, you have backups.

Each of these CBT domains for adult ADHD has a specific skill focus that works in tandem with the others. These CBT skills target ADHD and anxiety. They will help you deal with negative thoughts, frustrations, avoidance, pessimism, and other ways you might get stuck, so that you can get back on track rather than give up.

Cognitive Domain

The cognitive domain is the classic CBT skill of catching and assessing thoughts. A common thought pattern you might have is self-mistrust about your ability to start and finish tasks. ADHD makes these doubts more personal. For example, you might think, *I know I can do this. I don't trust I'll do it.* As you do the workbook exercises and employ these skills in your life, your changed outlooks and corresponding actions will promote greater self-trust and self-efficacy. These are principal cognitive objectives. Your self-trust also benefits from encouraging a mindset of *enough-ness* versus one of *less than* when dealing with tasks or people. Enough-ness mindsets address the fact you'll not always be at your best (or in the mood) but are good enough and have enough focus to engage and follow through on reasonable objectives, including facing anxiety.

Here is a brief list of common distortions observed in adults with ADHD.

PERFECTIONISM

Perfectionism isn't really a distorted thought, but it arises as a form of all-or-nothing thinking. For example, you might think, *If I'm not perfect, I've failed.* Perfectionism was the number-one endorsed adult ADHD distortion in a study by our group (Strohmeier et al. 2016). I've observed that adults with ADHD often face *front-end* perfectionism. For example, you might think, *I must be in the mood for a task, and circumstances must be just right. Otherwise, I cannot start it.* Adults with ADHD frequently use this type of thinking to justify procrastination. In this context, perfectionism is an attempt at emotion regulation: *If I can do this task perfectly and get it done now, it won't "hurt" as much.* Perfectionism is an unrealistic expectation that itself is anxiety-provoking and typically results in escape-avoidance. We will explore perfectionism in more detail in chapter 5.

ALL-OR-NOTHING THINKING

All-or-nothing thinking involves viewing matters in either/or, black/white categories without factoring in the gray areas. A common example when coping with ADHD is judging a single setback as evidence a coping tool doesn't work, such as thinking, *To-do lists don't work for me because I misplace them,* rather than finding ways to customize the skills. Even when things don't work out, there is usually a more reasonable, helpful middle-ground mindset to consider that promotes coping.

EMOTIONAL REASONING

The distortion of emotional reasoning shows up when your outlook is based solely on your feelings. You might think something like *If it feels bad, it is bad, so don't do it,* which is complementary to *I must be in the mood.* Emotional reasoning also appears in self-critical labeling, like *I feel like a failure, I feel stupid,* or *I feel like I'm a disappointment.* Reassessing your distorted thoughts includes considering how they connect with your emotions. This can help you think about things differently and accept and guide your feelings accordingly.

MAGNIFICATION/MINIMIZATION

Magnification involves blowing things out of proportion, for example, with anxieties. You might think, *This is the worst!* Minimization shortchanges your skills and ability to cope. For instance, you might think, *I can't handle this.* When facing tasks you don't want to do, you are likely to magnify all the possible negative aspects. This negativity triggers anxiety and stress. At the same time, you are likely to minimize your skills and ability to face the tasks and make progress. A typical middle-ground mindset, such as *This project is work but doable,* can help you face your ugh apprehension. Often, you'll find that a project usually goes better than anticipated once you get started.

COMPARATIVE THINKING

Social comparison, judging yourself based on how you match up with others, is part of human nature. It helps you discover your talents and acknowledge things that aren't your strong suits. Unfair comparisons, however, can magnify your shortcomings and minimize your competencies. Adults with ADHD are notoriously bad comparers. You can too easily cherry-pick admirable behaviors and characteristics you see in others (especially people without ADHD) and sour cherry–pick from your ADHD-related challenges in ways that leave you feeling discouraged and second-rate, or less than. Change occurs when you refocus on your goals and steps to improve and see yourself making progress.

POSITIVE THOUGHTS

Yes, positive thoughts can be distorted. They often appear as justifications for escape-avoidance. You plan to focus on a have-to priority, but another option arises. Unhelpful positive thoughts justify your switch to the less wise option: *I'll do this first, and then I'll be in the mood for the priority.* Other common examples include *I can do one more thing before I must leave* or *I work best at the last minute.* Most often, these off-task thoughts lead to procrastination and lateness.

Reflection

Record examples of the distortions above that resonate with you and any other distorted thoughts you notice.

_____

_____

_____

_____

_____

_____

_____

_____

Behavioral Domain

The behavioral domain of CBT focuses on what you choose to do and not do, how your actions align with your goals and values, and how you engage with and follow through on goals. Getting started and following through on tasks, instead of defaulting to escape-avoidance, is the main behavior that's targeted. The behavioral domain emphasizes using ADHD-adapted CBT coping skills that will help you turn your intentions into actions. These coping skills will also help you face anxiety associated with your intentions. Starting a work assignment when you're not in the mood or enacting a plan to handle several nerve-wracking duties, for example, are exposure steps for facing ADHD-related stress and anxiety. In terms of accepting and working through anxiety, changing your behavior to cope with overwhelm, social rejection anxiety, and other types of anxiety also falls within the behavioral domain.

Reflection

Write down examples of various tasks, chores, or obligations that you typically avoid or procrastinate on despite trying not to. Also note any ADHD-related coping strategies that you avoid using or that you've tried and abandoned.

_____

_____

_____

_____

_____

_____

_____

Emotional Domain

The emotional domain of CBT addresses your relationship with your feelings and your ability to accept them at the same time as you modify them. Sometimes this entails turning up your emotional dial, like gearing up to start a task. Sometimes this means turning down your emotional dial, like soothing stress and worry. The main emotional skill objective in CBT for adult ADHD centers on accepting and managing feelings of discomfort, chiefly the unpleasant feelings from the adult ADHD–anxiety connection.

Reflection

CBT focuses on the connection of thoughts, feelings, and behaviors. List some situations where you have noticed feelings of anxiety, stress, or other discomforts that interfere with your engagement and follow-through. Some of these might be reasons you picked up this workbook.

_____

_____

_____

_____

_____

_____

_____

Implementation Domain

The implementation domain of CBT narrowly focuses on skills for turning plans into actions. The skills in this workbook are overarchingly implementation focused. Managing adult ADHD is a performance issue that requires transitions from being off task to being on task. There are research-based coping statements designed to achieve this, which we will apply to ADHD. Their formal name is *implementation intention strategies*. The specific format is: "If/When I do or face (behavior/situation) X, then I will respond with (goal-focused behavior) Y" (Gollwitzer and Oettingen 2016). This is a useful strategy for getting started on a task or handling transitions between tasks. An example implementation statement might be, "If I open the dishwasher, then I will unload the top rack." Using the example of procrastination on a report, an implementation statement might be, "If I reread the last paragraph I wrote yesterday, then I will write for thirty minutes."

Reflection

Implementation statements are particularly helpful for initiating tasks, especially standalone tasks that you never get around to, or getting back on task after a distraction. Write out some implementation statements you can use.

_____

_____

_____

_____

_____

_____

Interpersonal Domain

The interpersonal domain of CBT focuses on how you define and fulfill your roles in relationships. This includes employing coping skills in relationship-enhancing ways. Self-compassion is a skill in this domain, because it involves your relationship with yourself. Chapter 6 explores interpersonal skills, such as assertiveness/self-advocacy, in detail. These CBT skills will help you fulfill your various obligations in your different life roles, balancing your needs with those of others.

Reflection

Look back on your previous Reflection responses. Which goals and examples involve your relationships and roles with others, such as at work or home? Note how you hope the workbook skills will help your relationships.

_____

_____

_____

_____

_____

_____

_____

_____

SAP Plan

The three-part coping action plan that I mentioned in the introduction, the SAP plan, offers a way to reframe your intentions so that you can turn them into actions. *SAP* stands for *specific, actionable,* and *pivot points*. The overarching idea is to take valued plans and goals that are broad and vague, such as coping better with adult ADHD, and boil them down into specific, actionable steps that you trust yourself to implement at targeted times (targeted pivot points) in your day. Here are more details about each step.

Be Specific

The first step of the SAP plan is to be *specific*. You probably have some broad, aspirational goals, such as better time management and reduced procrastination (covered in chapters 4 and 5). These objectives make perfect sense. Worded as such, though, they're daunting propositions, like getting in shape. Specificity is a foundation that involves defining precise, smaller, more immediately relevant examples of your objectives, such as completing an overdue assignment or on-time arrival at work tomorrow. From this foundation, you can use the same skills for other purposes. For example, you procrastinate on the small stuff—unloading the dishwasher—the same way you do on the big stuff—an overdue work assignment. When you focus on specifics for the little stuff, you're practicing the very skills you need for the big stuff.

Describe Tasks in Actionable Steps

The second step of the SAP plan is to describe tasks in *actionable,* or doable, steps. In the first step, you define an objective in specific terms, such as completing an overdue assignment or on-time arrival to work tomorrow. These are good intentions, but ADHD's not a knowledge problem. It's a performance problem. In the second step, you outline your specific intentions with specific steps that you believe you can do when and where you intend to do them. This is the point of performance. The actionable steps are not unlike the steps in a recipe. For example, you might identify the next step to take with the tardy report or changes in your morning routine to get out the door earlier for work. Seeing a task as both specific and doable is a cognitive reframe to foster self-trust that you'll take the first step.

Implement at Targeted Pivot Points

The third step of the SAP plan is to implement specific, and actionable tasks at targeted *pivot points.* Pivot points refer to transition points where you can actively shape the course of your day. Examples of targeted pivot points include a scheduled time in the evening to work on the overdue report or an earlier wake-up time to help you get ready for work on time. The idea follows the common observation that once you get started, you're more likely to keep going.

The SAP plan is effective for both ADHD and anxiety. Such transitions represent vulnerable points where anxiety can swoop in and conspire with ADHD to lure you into deserting your plans: *You really don't want to do this task right now.* However, steering through these transitions provides opportunities to get the most out of your coping skills.

Reflection

Select one of your goals in the workbook or another task you're facing and use the SAP plan to define it in specific, actionable terms and designate a specific pivot point in your day when you will implement it.

_____

_____

_____

_____

_____

_____

_____

_____

_____

Evaluate and Bounce Back

The SAP plan and the five domains of CBT provide a framework for addressing ADHD and its effects and crafting coping plans you trust yourself to implement. Since the relapse rate for ADHD coping slipups is 100 percent, this framework also helps you look back and figure out where and how you slipped up. You can use this information and the framework to bounce back using specific steps, instead of relying on the general notion of working harder next time to not procrastinate.

The other side of such reverse engineering is to give yourself due credit when you determine *I handled that as well as I could, and it's still a win for me.* It's important to acknowledge your successes and improvements as well as trusting your skills and aptitudes that you can call forth in future situations. This is an example of building flexible, helpful mindsets.

Summary

This chapter was a satellite view of CBT for adult ADHD. But CBT in action happens at the street-level view. It works by taking on specific, real-world problems, intentions, and other personally meaningful matters. The skills are designed to empower you to see and face them to the best of your abilities. Chapter 3 details how to put these elements together into a coping framework you'll practice and use throughout the rest of this workbook and beyond.

Approach Any Situation with a Coping Framework

In this chapter, you'll use CBT principles to address the effects of the adult ADHD–anxiety connection. You'll then use these skills to work through it—or over it, around it, under it, or any other direction that gets you to where you want to go. This process works best when you apply it to the life situations and settings that led you to pick up this workbook.

Keep in mind that these exercises take practice. Your adult ADHD–anxiety connection has had a big head start and is a well-oiled machine by now, which was one of Kelly's frustrations. Kelly was diagnosed with ADHD after almost failing out of college. Medications helped her get through college, but once out of school she avoided the rigid time demands of traditional office work, moving between flexible, low-demand jobs. Needing more security as a solo parent, she landed an administrative assistant job at a local college. She sought CBT for help with the stress of balancing work, parenthood, and adult life. For example, she needed better time-management skills. Medication helped with her focus, but she lacked coping skills.

I'll say the same thing to you that I said to Kelly, which is to be patient with yourself and the process. There will be slipups. The coping strategies provide a systematic way to review slipups, reverse engineer them, and understand what went awry. These actions will help you rebound and get back on track.

How to Reduce Stress: A CBT Practice Example

I'm guessing you might be having an *I don't want to do this* reaction to workbook exercises. Maybe you scanned the table of contents, flipped through some pages, and thought, *Time management, procrastination, nothing new here. This is like all the other ADHD books. What's the return policy?*

This skeptical reaction makes sense based on your genuine experiences and frustrations with ADHD. In fact, it's your anxiety protecting you from the risk of more frustrations. The skills you'll practice for managing your ADHD will help you successfully face and dilute such anxiety associations, cope better, and reduce stress. You just might find a different spin on an old coping skill that inspires you to give it another try.

Practice

Answer the following questions using a daily planner as an example of a coping tool. (We'll talk about daily planners in chapter 4.) If you already use a planner, pick a different coping tool. Each section is a CBT domain from chapter 2 and has prompts to guide you. To get you started, there are example replies using Kelly's reaction to planners.

Situation

Think about using a daily planner as a coping tool.

Take a moment to consider your motivation for the task at hand. Why do you want to do it in the first place? Once clear, determine your first steps to engage with it.

Example: It's recommended I use a planner. My next action steps are to read the rest of this chapter, do the exercises, and then read the time-management chapter.

Your response: _____

_____

_____

What is your goal for using a daily planner?

Example: I want to see if the planner and other skills help me better manage ADHD and be more on top of things with less stress.

Your response: _____

_____

_____

Cognitive Domain

Consider your first thoughts or reactions to using a planner.

How could they affect your goal?

Example: This is nothing new, it won't work, and I'm too busy to waste time. This is my assumption. I'll see if this time is different.

Your response: _____

_____

_____

How might your thoughts about using a planner be distorted? How can you counter any distortions?

Example: My reaction is a negative prediction before I've even tried using a planner. Lots of people have recommended trying a planner. I'm willing to read about using a planner.

Your response: _____

_____

_____

What is a thought or mindset to help you follow through with your goal of using a planner?

Example: I can keep an open mind, do the steps, and see how it works. I'm more motivated to do this now than before.

Your response: _____

_____

_____

Emotional Domain

Consider your worries, discomforts, and uncertainties about your goal of using a planner.

What anxieties, other emotions, or physical sensations do you notice?

Example: I'm feeling nervous, frustrated, and a little angry. I feel tension in my shoulders and a little queasiness in my gut.

Your response: _____

_____

_____

What do you think these emotions are telling you or signaling to you?

Example: My stress is telling me to stop wasting valuable time, because I don't think this will help me. I'm also worried about failing and losing my job.

Your response: _____

_____

_____

How could you personalize and label these feelings to help you accept and work with them?

Example: Frustration is my "I hate planning" feeling. I also have ADHD stress from working so hard to keep up with life. I can notice the feeling, take deep breaths, and keep going. Some of what I feel might be hope that this might help.

Your response: _____

_____

_____

Behavioral Domain

Consider how behavior could help you use a planner and support your goal for using a planner.

What are specific actions you can take next to follow through?

Example: After I read the time-management chapter, I'll get a planner and use it for a month.

Your response: _____

_____

_____

How could escape-avoidance interfere with your action steps? How would you handle it?

Example: I could get overwhelmed researching planners and give up. I'll find a basic, good-enough planner.

Your response: _____

_____

_____

Why is your goal worth the hassle?

Example: I'll try the planner to be more organized for my daughter and me. It's worth the hassle to be less stressed and more on top of things.

Your response: _____

_____

_____

Implementation Domain

Formulate an "If/When X, then Y" implementation plan for your goal.

What is your implementation plan for using a planner that supports your goal?

Example: When I get a planner, I'll spend ten minutes entering work meetings and soccer games for this month.

Your response: _____

_____

_____

Interpersonal Domain

Think about the effects of using a planner and your goal on yourself in your various roles and on your relationships with others.

How does using a planner and your goal involve or affect others in your life?

Example: I want to be a good example for my daughter and aware of her schedule. I want to be organized at work and be seen as reliable.

Your response: _____

_____

_____

In terms of relationships, how can you stay on track with your goal?

Example: I will prioritize times with my daughter and say no to requests that conflict with them. I'll ask for help at work if I feel overscheduled or stressed.

Your response: _____

_____

_____

How can you practice self-compassion using a planner and moving toward your goal?

Example: I'll be patient with myself, focus on my progress, and learn from any mistakes.

Your response: _____

_____

_____

_____

Practice Summary

How did it go? The exercise works on several levels.

First, slowing things down to write out your thoughts, feelings, and behavior plans externalizes information. From there, you can see your thoughts without having to hold them in mind. The writing is an exposure task for matters that elicit anxiety and ugh feelings. The exercise is an emotional distancing exercise that allows you to sit with your feelings.

Second, exercises like this allow you to pause, reflect on your reactions, and then *proflect,* which means envisioning yourself in the future carrying out actions aligned with your present objectives. It's a mental dress rehearsal for your desired mindset, emotional management, and action plan. Considering at least one other way to think about and handle a situation doubles your options. Time and contemplation of your discomfiting feelings helps quiet them, at least a little bit. You can imagine actions. All raise the odds of turning your intentions into actions. These processes are enhanced by devising an implementation statement and considering the relevance of your plan for relationships.

Summary

Give yourself credit. You did a lot in this chapter. You were introduced to the CBT framework and used it in a way that complements the skills you'll practice in later chapters. CBT is goal focused, and you need a plan for achieving a goal. This requires you to organize your behavior over time, which is the essence of time management. In chapter 4, you'll learn about time-management tools and strategies.

CHAPTER 4

Reduce Overwhelm with Time Management

Managing ADHD in adulthood is like trying to wrestle an octopus—underwater and blindfolded. It's impossible to change everything all at once, and it's likely overwhelming to think about making big changes. Consequently, as you practice and implement the skills and strategies you learn from this workbook, I recommend that you focus on small matters to generate early successes.

For example, you might take on a small task like submitting one overdue expense report. Perhaps you want to catch up on your backlog of emails, but instead start with yesterday's inbox. If you find grocery shopping overwhelming, do a trial run with a small list of staple items.

Each of these steps is a building block for assembling your repertoire of ADHD coping skills. You'll still face stress and anxiety, but in smaller doses. Remember the SAP plan of specific, actionable steps implemented at targeted pivot points? This strategy can be applied to all sorts of matters. This chapter focuses on time management.

Time management is an issue that's anxiety-provoking for many adults with ADHD. ADHD makes it difficult and hence stressful to juggle duties and responsibilities, both your have-tos and the want-tos. Even the prospect of confronting them can be a recipe for worry and overwhelm. This is why you need a way to face your days that promotes engagement and follow-through but that ultimately reduces stress. This is the essence of time management—how you organize your time, effort, and energy, and thereby pace yourself across time.

Facing the Need for Time Management

Time management is the most common executive-function problem cited by adults with ADHD (Barkley 2012). It's essentially how you *spend yourself* and pace yourself over an hour, day, week, or any stretch of time to accomplish your aims (Ramsay and Rostain 2015a).

A planner or calendar of some sort is a foundational time-management tool. Getting started with a planner entails the accounting of what you want to or must do in a day. The most common entries involve duties and appointments for work, school, and family and social commitments. Planners can help track and complete other activities, including those that promote well-being, like exercise and health-related appointments. It's the recreation and well-being plans, though, that often are sacrificed when dealing with undone tasks that follow you around like an ominous cloud, stressing you out and sapping your peace of mind.

Reflection

Which of these statements sound familiar? Add below any other similar statements that resonate with you.

I make great plans, but I don't follow them.

I have a schedule and list of things to do, but then I don't use them.

I get off to a good start, but then I get off track, and my plan goes awry.

I'm busy all day but don't get anything done.

I mismanage my time with distractions and end up with no time for myself.

I know people busier than I am who seem to get more done in less time.

Add any similar statements that resonate with you.

_____

_____

_____

_____

Reflection

What are some life balance or well-being activities that you never seem to have time for, but you could schedule?

_____ _____

_____ _____

_____ _____

_____ _____

_____ _____

_____ _____

It makes sense that time management is problematic for most adults with ADHD. It involves keeping track of commitments, juggling different roles and duties, and monitoring your effort through each day and across each week. Time doesn't stop when you hit the snooze button in bed or scroll on your phone to escape stress. The time-management tools and strategies reviewed here will help you face your day, customize your schedule, and outfit it with specific, actionable tasks, along with designated time slots furnishing pivot points to promote implementation.

Daily Planner

Yes. I know. I know. A daily planner is *the* cliché ADHD coping tool. That's the reason your (and Kelly's) skepticism about the planner are likely reflected in chapter 3's practice exercise.

Resistance to planning is a common one: making structured plans is stressful and anxiety-provoking. Many adults with ADHD see planning as a setup for failure. You'll resist planning for what you'll do at, say, 3 p.m. unless you know right now that you'll be in the mood later (you won't). As a result, there's a temptation to wing it and figure out your day as it unfolds.

Bear in mind that because winging it is a high cognitive-load endeavor, it's tiring (Levitin 2014; Mlodinow 2022). Such fatigue reduces the quality of your decision-making and impulse control, which makes you prone to seek out easier, more immediately enjoyable distractions (Paul 2021). This is a tendency that ADHD magnifies. Winging it works against managing your ADHD and anxiety.

Having at least a semblance of a plan for your day, such as what you'll do before lunch versus after lunch, involves facing smaller helpings of stress now to reduce larger-later stress and anxiety. Even the following bare-bones plan is a first step toward implementation.

Here are steps for using a planner to map out your days.

Start with Known Commitments

You get twenty-four hours in a day, one hundred sixty-eight hours in a week. Wall calendars and other planners, including digital, are merely rows and columns divvying up time increments that allow you to *see* time. You can then earmark how you want to use the resulting slots. (You can accomplish the same thing using a whiteboard, a spreadsheet, or a sheet of paper.)

Externalizing time is especially important for adults with ADHD because it allows you to work with time but without the mental energy needed to hold it in mind—and the risk of it falling out, which it will (Levitin 2014). A daily planner helps you portion-control time and its flow during a day and across days. It's like having a $24 daily budget and $168 for the week.

As a first step, populate your planner with known obligations, such as doctor appointments and work meetings. You determine the level of granularity that works for you. You might also reserve times for lunch, dog-walking, homework, and other such tasks. I recommend scheduling protected time, such as buffer times for commuting, your go-to-bed and wake-up times, exercise, and other recurring events.

Sounds logical. However, such planned expectations, even of your making, still might trigger stress and anxiety. These might be subtle ughs, or a palpable no-way, gut-level resistance when looking at a day or week outlined in this fashion. These reactions are the battle of thoughts *I can do this* versus *I can't* or *I don't want to.* Facing this discomfort when outlining your day is the norm and can be framed as an investment toward coping with the adult ADHD–anxiety connection. A helpful reframe is that your planning anxiety is the revving up of energy to face the priority task of starting your day.

If you still feel resistant to using a planner, reread the exercise in chapter 3 and work through the CBT items to review a planner's value to you.

How Do I Do What I Planned to Do Today?

After setting out a plan, the blueprint of your day, the focus shifts to implementation: what now, and what next? These steps echo the well-worn but nonetheless wise advice to break down tasks into small steps. This ADHD task-implementation skill is a buy-one-get-one deal, representing progressive exposure to face and defuse anxiety vis-à-vis this one-step-at-a-time approach.

Another way to reduce stress when formulating your daily plan is to reserve time for breaks and other open slots in your day. Pockets of downtime provide energizing breaks in the day. Keeping your plans realistic improves your chances of experiencing positive feelings of accomplishment as you make progress throughout the day and the satisfaction of reaching the end of a productive day (Hofmann 2016).

The daily planner is a versatile tool for use in your personal life. It's helpful not only for chores and errands, but also for dinner reservations, exercise, and playdates. Even interactions in relationships can be defined by tasks tracked using your planner. We'll revisit this in chapter 6.

===================== Practice =====================

Let's look at an example of a day's plan to get you started. This is a more detailed schedule than you might need. You can download the "Daily Planner" worksheet at http://www.newharbinger.com/52434.

Daily Planner Example

12 a.m.	Sleep
1 a.m.	Sleep
2 a.m.	Sleep
3 a.m.	Sleep
4 a.m.	Sleep
5 a.m.	Sleep
6 a.m.	Sleep/6:30 a.m. alarm, shower/dress, let dog out
7 a.m.	Breakfast, go to train station
8 a.m.	Commute to work, arrive at office
9 a.m.	Review planner, check/respond to emails
10 a.m.	Staff meeting until 10:45 a.m.
11 a.m.	Prospecting for new clients, follow up with inquiries

12 p.m.	Lunch, review emails from the morning
1 p.m.	Start work on monthly report, use last month as template, update with new information
2 p.m.	Keep working on monthly report until 2:30 p.m., do required online training
3 p.m.	Discretionary: keep working on monthly report or other matters that may have come up today
4 p.m.	Wrap up admin matters from the day, review notes from meetings, set tomorrow's daily plan
5 p.m.	Walk to train station, commute home
6 p.m.	Arrive home, unpack, walk dog, prepare dinner
7 p.m.	Finish dinner, clean up, jog on treadmill
8 p.m.	Downtime, putter around, read/TV, etc.
9 p.m.	More downtime
10 p.m.	Hang out, pack work bag, make lunch, let dog out
11 p.m.	In bed 11:30 p.m., read if not tired right away

Daily Planner for You

Now fill out a daily schedule for yourself that reflects a typical day.

12 a.m.	
1 a.m.	
2 a.m.	
3 a.m.	
4 a.m.	
5 a.m.	
6 a.m.	
7 a.m.	
8 a.m.	
9 a.m.	
10 a.m.	
11 a.m.	

12 p.m.	
1 p.m.	
2 p.m.	
3 p.m.	
4 p.m.	
5 p.m.	
6 p.m.	
7 p.m.	
8 p.m.	
9 p.m.	
10 p.m.	
11 p.m.	

You might need a planner with smaller time increments, such as fifteen- or thirty-minute slots, or you might have a job, such as in a hospital emergency department, where the best-laid plans change without notice. Nevertheless, a planner allows you to organize intentions and increase the likelihood of implementation. Include unstructured days, like weekends or holidays, in your planner to get the most out of them.

How Do I Make My Daily Planner Work for Me?

A good habit and implementation step is to review your planner the night before or at the start of a day: *If I open my planner, then I'll review and update it for 600 seconds.* Reframing time in this way can make tasks seem more doable. This run-through promotes follow-through. During this review, you can eyeball times for specific tasks like projects, errands, or breaks. These times spell out your day as a series of pivot points. Another planner function is to decrease worry and stress. You spend time looking over your day divided up, including breaks and end points for activities, and see that it is doable.

Your planner is also a record of your accomplishments, which you likely too often dismiss. A common thought pattern you might notice is making "yes, but" statements about your feats that discount the positive—for example, *Yes, I was on time for work, but I didn't accomplish much.* Your planner provides data to better gauge your day—for example, *I faded at the end, but I still accomplished a lot.*

Information gleaned from your planner can help you make adjustments. For example, you might discover that you need to depart earlier for your doctor appointments due to traffic, or that mornings are good slots for more complex tasks, like monthly reports.

Practice

Let's have you use your CBT skills with your daily planner by answering the following questions.

Cognitive Domain

What thoughts or doubts am I having about the daily planner that might interfere with using it?

_____

_____

_____

What is a helpful mindset about using it, and how it might help me?

_____

_____

_____

Are my plans and expectations specific and realistic?

_____

_____

_____

Behavioral Domain

What sort of planner works best for me?

_____

_____

_____

When will I spend time setting up and reviewing my plan for a day?

_____

_____

_____

Emotional Domain

What worries or other feelings do I notice about the planner?

_____

_____

_____

Are any of these feelings self-protective discomfort based on past frustrations and uncertainty?

_____

_____

_____

How can I accept and tolerate these discomforts as normal and still use the planner?

_____

_____

_____

Implementation Domain

What is my "If/When X, then Y" strategy for setting up and reviewing my plan?

_____

_____

_____

What is my "If/When X, then Y" strategy for keeping track of new commitments and plans?

_____

_____

_____

Interpersonal Domain

What times do I want to reserve for self-care?

_____

_____

_____

What times do I want to reserve for people at work or in my personal life?

_____

_____

_____

How will I practice self-compassion with my planner use?

_____

_____

_____
_____

To-Do List

To-do lists have a bad reputation for not working, usually because they're too ambitious. A to-do list is not meant to be an inventory of everything you must do. Toting around such a monstrous list is sure to stir up anxiety and resistance to using it. By the same token, merely jotting down a task on a list won't magically make it happen.

The to-do list is your planner's companion tool. It's a doable task list—two to maybe five items. Err on the low side until you learn what you can handle. Reserve this list for matters that fall outside the flow of your typical day but that require extra attention and effort to remember and execute. Thus, a college student wouldn't list "attend classes," but might add "attend Dr. Rosenfield's office hours." Your to-do lists can contain tasks or habits that benefit from reminders like "go for a walk during lunch."

Additional tips for making to-do lists more ADHD-friendly are to assign tasks specific times or pivot points, like "get milk on way home." The SAP plan elements of specific, actionable task descriptions (like "schedule appointment for oil change when the mechanic opens at 8 a.m.") help, too.

To-do lists are meant to be portable and easily accessible. Some people like to use an app on their phone. Others prefer a paper list, which provides a tangible reminder. Use whatever works for you.

Practice

Let's look at a to-do list example and then have you try one. You can download this "To-Do List" worksheet at http://www.newharbinger.com/52434.

Example To-Do List

Task	When It Will Be Done
Email human resources about reimbursement for my credentialing exam	10:45 a.m. after staff meeting
Make online appointment for doctor	4 p.m. during admin time
Give dog heartworm medication	6 p.m. before dog walk

Your Practice To-Do List

Task	When It Will Be Done

Setting Priorities

Setting priorities can influence how you order tasks in your day's plan. For example, you can divide time (and thus tasks) into now and not-now categories. One danger is being too now-focused to the detriment of tasks offering larger-later payoffs, which is a common pitfall for adults with ADHD. If a task isn't immediately absorbing (defusing a bomb), it too often resides in the not-now category. This makes it tempting to disregard it (scheduling that dental visit) until you face a deadline or compelling now signal (sore tooth). Setting priorities takes the not-now tasks and creates "but when?" slots for them in your planner and often on your to-do list.

You may face now/not-now tasks when a matter is carried over on your to-do lists for days. A rapidly approaching deadline may lead you to explode into full-on hyperfocus and high energy. This happens because anxiety stimulates your body and motivates you with the prospect of a missed deadline or other now-palpable worries.

Setting priorities helps prevent last-minute alarms. It doesn't mean that the most important task always gets first dibs. Think of the planner as displaying the real estate of your day. What are your most valuable properties (time slots)? For some adults with ADHD, the morning is a valuable plot due to being fully rested and benefiting from morning medications. On the other hand, many adults with ADHD are wired for productivity later in the day or evening (Hallowell and Ratey 2021), which frees up earlier times in the day for other matters (Mlodinow 2022). This is a place where you can tailor time-management skills to optimize your strengths.

After committing the high-end properties in your day's schedule for priority tasks, fill in other tasks and activities in open slots thoughtfully. For example, if you work on a report first thing in your day, next take on a task with a lower or different cognitive load. This is similar to circuit training with a sequence of aerobic and anaerobic exercises training different body systems. While one system is being taxed, the other is resting.

Practice

Let's run through your coping strategies for to-do lists and setting priorities.

Cognitive Domain

What thoughts or doubts am I having about to-do lists that might interfere with using them?

_____

_____

_____

What is a helpful mindset about using them and how they might help me?

_____

_____

_____

Are my expectations specific and realistic?

_____

_____

_____

Behavioral Domain

What format will I use for my to-do list to make it user-friendly for me?

_____

_____

_____

What time of day should I reserve for higher-priority tasks?

_____

_____

_____

When will I review my to-do list to make it a daily habit? ?

_____

_____

_____

Emotional Domain

What worries or other feelings do I notice about to-do lists?

_____

_____

_____

Are any of these feelings self-protective discomforts based on past frustrations and uncertainty?

_____

_____

_____

How can I accept and tolerate these discomforts as normal and still use a to-do list?

_____

_____

_____

Implementation Domain

What is my "If/When *X*, then *Y*" strategy for setting up and reviewing my to-do list?

_____

_____

_____

What is my "If/When *X*, then *Y*" strategy for my to-do list tasks?

_____

_____

_____

Interpersonal Domain

What is at least one task on my to-do list for self-care?

_____

_____

_____

What is at least one task on my to-do list related to a work relationship and another for a personal relationship?

_____

_____

_____
_____

Summary

The daily planner and a to-do list provide the scaffolding of your day. These tools help you set priorities and schedule tasks in ways that set you up for success. The time investment to create, review, and update them can pay off by reducing stress and anxiety. These tools also promote follow-through. You gain the payoff of feeling on top of your schedule.

A common CBT treatment goal for adults with ADHD is to not only set up such daily plans but also to implement them. This chapter focused on the setup. Chapter 5 focuses on taming the predator that feeds on plans before they hatch: procrastination.

CHAPTER 5

Build Trust in Yourself to Overcome Procrastination

Barry's procrastination on his work project was a classic ADHD example that might have felt familiar to you. He had a plan for the project, but he kept putting it off until the anxiety and stress of facing it was overcome by his fear of having nothing to give his boss—not now became *now!* Barry paid the price with a stressful, sleepless night, which took him days to fully recover from.

You may have paid a financial price for procrastination, such as credit card late fees or penalties for unpaid taxes. (Financial costs associated with ADHD are called the ADHD tax, which we'll talk about in chapter 6.) Lost opportunities might stem from missed application deadlines, poor grades, or disappointing performance reviews. Even when doing something other than your intended plan, you might not really be doing anything fulfilling. You're likely just treading time, avoiding the stress of facing the priority task.

Procrastination is the number-one problem I see with adults with ADHD. One definition of procrastination is "to voluntarily delay an intended course of action despite expecting to be worse off for the delay" (Steel 2007, 66). Although you know that you have the ability to handle a task, your anxiety undermines your belief that you can face the boring details and tedious steps necessary to persist and complete the task. In turn, the resulting doubt strengthens your tendency for self-mistrust and escape-avoidance (Bandura 1997; Ramsay 2020).

Impulsivity also plays a role in procrastination (Steel 2007). All it takes is a quick, unthinking moment, like refreshing a social media account, to make it even easier to procrastinate.

=============================== Reflection ===============================

List examples of tasks, chores, and any duties you're likely to put off for later.

_____   _____

_____   _____

_____   _____

_____   _____

_____   _____

What Is Procrastivity?

The goal to work harder to not procrastinate is not specific and actionable enough to succeed. Fortunately, a particular form of procrastination, called procrastivity, offers clues we'll use as tools to overcome procrastination.

Procrastivity is a term for when you avoid a high-priority but complex or tedious task by working on any other tasks that you're suddenly motivated to do instead of what you planned, such as errands or chores. This is ultimately self-defeating. It's also known as *productive procrastination* because at least you did something fruitful. Something's better than nothing, right?

Here are some examples of procrastivity (see Ramsay 2020 for an in-depth review). You convince yourself to mow the lawn instead of working on your income taxes as you planned. You persuade yourself that yardwork will put you in the right mood to face the IRS. Or maybe you organize your desk rather than face a work or school assignment.

Procrastivity tasks are like a Trojan horse arriving under the guise of productivity. However, they really are another form of escape-avoidance. Let's look at some common features of procrastivity tasks and then talk about how you can repurpose these features to stay on track with your main objectives. These features:

- tend to be hands-on, manual

- have clear, actionable steps for getting started

- offer a reasonable guess for how long they'll take

- let you see and maintain the progress you've made

- provide a clear endpoint at which you're done with the task

These features of procrastivity tasks can be applied to your goals to face anxiety, more consistently implement plans, and overcome procrastination. You might dismiss these coping suggestions as tricks. Yes, absolutely, they're tricks for getting engaged. Engagement is the chief behavioral objective. Self-mistrust and ugh feelings are your brain's tricks for procrastination in the first place. These countermeasures are antiprocrastination coping tools that you'll use in an antiprocrastination plan, which we'll cover next.

Your Antiprocrastination Plan

As part of building an antiprocrastination plan, answer the following questions:

- What am I *not* doing?

- Why do it?

- What's its value to me?

The first step in overcoming procrastination is clarifying exactly what it is that you set out to do but are *not* doing. What is *it*? Define *it*. You might be overwhelmed by what appears to be a straightforward task, like "do homework." If you're facing three assignments, however, that's three distinct tasks—all with multiple subtasks. This kind of situation creates the stress reaction that makes you want to escape. If you're feeling overwhelmed, narrow your focus to a specific, doable *it* task, like completing one set of math problems.

"Why do *it*?" is the next question. This is a stop-and-think step to fend off your ADHD escape reflex. Asking "Why do it?" makes you pause and establish the benefits of facing it now. Even thinking about the task is cognitive exposure, a moment allowing you to lessen and defuse stress, anxiety, and ugh feelings.

"What's its value to *me*?" is the third question. This is your personal valuation of a task, your buy-in. You can consider your big-picture goals. For example, you need to finish your assignments to complete a class you need for graduation. You can also consider more immediate benefits. Imagining your future self is a helpful image. This might include imagining even two minutes after starting the task and the relief you'll feel once engaged. You can also imagine your later-in-the-day feeling, knowing that you already did what you set out to do. Sometimes the value of facing a task is knowing that you can do so when you need to. This builds your self-trust coping muscle.

Steps to Define Tasks

Adults without ADHD can handle broadly defined tasks ("clean house") because they can hold such plans in their mind's eye and mentally portion them into steps. This portioning is a "first this, then that" sequence of behaviors ("unload the dishwasher, load the dirty dishes, run it").

Difficulties holding in mind thoughts and images, sequences of steps, and time are executive-function problems. This is why you and other adults with ADHD benefit from writing out an outline of action steps for your task, at least enough to get you launched. The purpose of this visible sequence is to give you a behavioral script or recipe that promotes the coping thought *Even if I don't feel like it, I can do these steps.*

What Is the Smallest Step to Start?

The very first step in the sequence of steps is a crucial pivot point that gets special attention. It defines how you *touch* the task and move from not doing to doing. This step transforms your abstract plan into reality, your intention into action. Using the "clean up kitchen" example, the specific task might be "unload dishwasher" and the corresponding sequence of steps for doing so. The first launch step is "open dishwasher door." You could conceivably stop after performing this first step, but after touching the task you're much more likely to keep going.

Moving your body to a location where the task will be done is a good first step ("walk to kitchen"). These are steps are specific and actionable at tailor-made pivot points. You can perform them even while feeling discomfort from anxiety. They also function as exposure steps. Spoiler alert: you'll never, ever feel like doing certain work projects, homework, chores, or anything else you see as work (Jaffe 2013).

These tricks help you get engaged. Even though have-to tasks are effortful, the feeling of accomplishment is rewarding. We tend to underestimate how good such accomplishment, like completing tasks and solving problems (Hofmann 2016), feels because it is a delayed-reward feeling. That said, getting engaged in a small first step provides some relief, even if it's resignation: *Oh, all right, I might as well just do this.* You start feeling better once you begin.

The next issue to hammer out is the details of when, for how long, and where you'll do the task.

When Will I Do This?

The answer to "When?" is an appointment with yourself. On a specific day at a set time, you commit to doing the task. This precommitment reduces the cognitive load of figuring out your plan on the fly. Recording task appointments in your daily planner lets you offload and forget about them until the appointed time, rather than carrying them around in your mind as something you must do (Levitin 2014). What's more, the cognitive load from the back-and-forth thinking about *Should I do it now or later?* makes you susceptible to mental fatigue and now/not-now avoidance.

The enough-ness reframe we talked about in chapter 2 is helpful. This mindset promotes the idea that circumstances will likely be less than perfect but are more than adequate, sufficient, or enough to get started. Enough-ness is the idea that you have enough focus, energy, and efficacy to initiate your plan, and that you, too, are enough and capable. This counters the less-than self-view.

How Long Will I Spend on This?

You can counteract now/not-now thinking by creating a time-bounded task, setting both start and end-times for it.

Task-bounding, such as setting a minimum number of homework problems or other realistic quotas, is another tactic. A way to think about a bounded portion is to answer the question, "How much can I do, or how long can I last, if this task is as awful as I worry it could be?"

You probably recall times when you got on a roll and had freakishly long stretches of productivity (not including last-minute all-nighters), such as a four-hour work or chore stint. I'm guessing you didn't set out expecting to work for that long but caught and rode a wave of momentum. Thinking about a four-hour task is overwhelming, even for something you like doing. Instead, set up reasonable bounded plans. When possible, though, leave a buffer in the event you are motivated to keep going longer.

Where Will I Do This?

Choose where you'll do the task. Having a go-to place, such as your desk at home or a library, where you'll execute your plan adds actionable specificity to it. It creates a tailor-made pivot point and first step of getting there. With each successive step, you're facing and reducing anxiety and getting into work mode. You're also recruiting memories and task-promoting associations for the job at hand, even if your motivation is resignation (*[Long sigh] Let's just do this*).

What Is My Implementation Plan?

Your implementation plan is your implementation statement for a task (Gollwitzer and Oettingen 2016): "If/When I do or face (behavior/situation) X, then I will respond with (goal-focused behavior)

Y." Consider the elements of your task plan—what, why, when, where, and for how long—when creating your implementation statement.

Figuring out the elements of your task plan sets the stage for execution. Implementation plans are ideal for getting you started. They encapsulate the essential first step you can take to launch a task, such as "When I sit down at my desk, then I'll work on my report for thirty minutes." Implementation plans can also be used to reengage with a task after a break or an interruption, which are vulnerable times for escape.

Implementation plans can curtail unhelpful behaviors, too. For example, you might want to make "don't do this" plans that anticipate risks for escape-avoidance. If you're prone to impulsive online shopping, for instance, an implementation plan could be: "If I find myself shopping online, then I'll stop, pick up where I left off, and work until my task end-time."

Practicing Your Antiprocrastination Plan

Practice time! Let's give you a chance to try this on for size.

═══ Practice ═══

Using an example of procrastination relevant to your life, answer the following questions. You could use a recent example of when you procrastinated on a task or something you're facing now. You can download the "Outline Your Antiprocrastination Plan" worksheet with these questions at http://www.newharbinger.com/52434.

Define What You Intend to Do

Start by asking yourself the following three questions about what you intend to do.

What am I not doing? _____

_____

_____

Why do it? _____

_____

_____

What is its value to me? _____

_____

_____

Define the Task

Use the following steps to define the task.

What is the smallest step to start? _____

_____

_____

When will I do this? _____

_____

_____

How long will I spend on this? _____

_____

_____

Where will I do this? _____

_____

_____

What is my implementation plan? _____

_____

_____

_____

_____

How'd it go? You may find a favorite coping tip or two that work best for you, such as valuation, task-bounding, or implementation statements. For particularly challenging tasks, cycling through all the steps might be what works. This format also encourages you to figure out what happened whenever you find yourself procrastinating, so you can take corrective action going forward.

The next section is the CBT companion section of your antiprocrastination plan. It focuses on dealing with the barriers that can undermine your intention to not procrastinate.

How Do I Stick to My Task Plan?

You've practiced the CBT skills we're going to cover in this section. Now you're going to adapt them to procrastination. At some point, you've probably orchestrated a well-designed task plan. You were wholeheartedly committed to it for twenty-three hours and fifty-nine minutes—up until it was time to execute it. You probably felt an ugh feeling and wound up catching up on emails, tidying your desk, or cleaning the vegetable drawer in your refrigerator instead.

Because procrastination is such an important issue, I'm going to review procrastination-specific issues for each of the CBT skill domains and pose corresponding questions for you to answer as practice. You can download the "Stay Motivated with Your Antiprocrastination Plan" worksheet with a list of the questions for each CBT skills domain at http://www.newharbinger.com/52434.

Cognitive Domain: How Do I Think Myself Out of Tasks?

Many kinds of thoughts can interfere with engagement and follow-through, including task anticipation. I mentioned that front-end perfectionism—*If I can't be perfect or if circumstances aren't just right, then it's no use starting*—commonly sparks procrastination for adults with ADHD. Indeed, it's an *anti*-implementation "If/When X, then Y" statement. Front-end perfectionism is also spurred by your gut-level, task-related discomfort to anything you view as work.

Now consider the opposite implementation statement: "If circumstances are just right and I'm perfect, then I won't feel bad. I'll do the task quickly and painlessly and be done with it." Unfortunately, this unrealistic mindset puts words to feelings that trigger procrastination.

Trying to be perfect itself is anxiety-provoking. It makes you underestimate your ability to face and invest your discomfort to engage in the task—a step that when taken relieves discomfort. The goal is to harness your enough-ness to get started and achieve a more satisfying sense of accomplishment later.

Practice

Here are questions to steer your mindset and outlook away from procrastination and toward implementation and accomplishment. These prompts give you an opportunity to pause, write down, and assess your anticipations. This process helps you guide your outlook to be more aligned with your intentions and valuation. You can download the "Stay Motivated with Your Antiprocrastination Plan" worksheet with these questions at http://www.newharbinger.com /52434.

How am I thinking about my task plan?

_____

_____

_____

How might my thoughts be distorted or underestimate my abilities, my "enough-ness"?

_____

_____

_____

Can I tolerate and invest some discomfort to get started?

_____

_____

_____

What's the worst case for my task plan? Best case? Most likely case?

_____

_____

_____

What is a more helpful mindset for facing this task and its value to me?

_____

_____

_____

Your cognitive skills focus on normalizing and accepting discomforts while you cultivate self-trust to execute your plan and achieve results, including incremental ones. Being discomfort- and stress-free is not a necessary or even a desired precondition to engagement and follow-through. If it's something you don't care about, why would you want to do it? Let's now focus on dealing with escape behaviors that undermine your intentions.

Behavioral Domain: What Are My Escape Behaviors?

Temptations to procrastinate, like procrastivity and escape-avoidance, reside in the behavioral domain. Your antiprocrastination plan outlines tactics to make your priority tasks specific and actionable to be implemented at targeted pivot points. However, you also need to be prepared to face distractions that can easily lead to procrastination and knock you off track.

Practice

These questions will help you reflect on how to keep yourself engaged with your task plan versus giving in to procrastination. You can download the "Stay Motivated with Your Antiprocrastination Plan" worksheet with these questions at http://www.newharbinger.com/52434.

What are my typical escape behaviors? Digital distractions? Procrastivity tasks?

_____

_____

_____

How can I remove or handle temptations and distractions? Can I tolerate them?

_____

_____

_____

What are the action steps in my task plan that will most help me get engaged?

_____

_____

_____

How good will my future self feel when I start and follow my plan?

_____

_____

_____

Some of these questions relate to both the cognitive and emotional domains. Indeed, time-bounding and day/time/place scheduling are cognitive because they define tasks in specific, doable terms. The emotional domain deals more directly with overcoming potential barriers from anxiety feelings.

Emotional Domain: How Do My Feelings Interfere with Tasks?

Remember that a core feature of anxiety is intolerance of uncertainty—you're never 100 percent sure how plans will go—and adults with ADHD too often have seen things go poorly. Still, uncertainty is biased toward the negative (Tierney and Baumeister 2019) and undervalues the hopeful, optimistic side of things. The skills you're gaining here will help you more positively direct your life.

Facing unpleasant feelings starts with recognizing and naming them, their influence, and what they mean to you. Labeling emotions is an effective way to manage them because such cataloging dials down your brain's emotion system (Barrett et al. 2001; Brooks et al. 2017; Lieberman et al. 2007). This exercise will help you pinpoint feelings and work with them to stay on track, rather than dodging them with procrastination.

Practice

Below are questions to help you recognize and name your emotions. You can download the "Stay Motivated with Your Antiprocrastination Plan" worksheet with these questions at http://www .newharbinger.com/52434.

What am I feeling right now about my task plan?

_____

_____

_____

What emotion words describes my feelings?

_____

_____

_____

Is there a personalized label I could give my feelings? For example: "This is my 'I hate homework frustration.'"

_____

_____

_____

What are the bodily sensations associated with my emotions?

_____

_____

_____

What information are these emotions giving me? Is there a theme with these emotions, such as uncertainty or risk?

_____

_____

_____

_____

A mantra is words that you repeat to yourself, often to help you focus. Repeating a personal mantra can help you intentionally counteract unhelpful thoughts. The following example mantras can help you process feelings and persist on your task plan. After you read them, consider other ones that you may use.

- I can notice my feelings without trying to change them.

- These emotions feel unpleasant, but they are not harmful.

- I'm willing to accept these feelings even if I don't want to have them.

- Discomfort is normal when facing tasks that I don't want to do.

- Once I get started, I'll feel better.

You can reframe your discomforts and thoughts that interfere with your task plan by thinking of them like seasonal allergies or an itchy sweater, annoyances that needn't disrupt plans. It's behavioral follow-through that's the ultimate goal of antiprocrastination strategies. To this end, your implementation statement promotes behavioral engagement (and reengagement when you drift off task).

Implementation Domain: How Do I Move from Not Doing to Doing?

This implementation domain is part of the antiprocrastination plan. To get started, revisit your "If/When X, then Y" implementation statement. Then think about how your implementation plans can help you avoid temptations or get back on track after a distraction or a break.

=== Practice ===

Think of a few situations you might face with the task where "If/When) X, then Y" implementation statements might be relevant to you. Write them out so you have them handy. You can download the "Stay Motivated with Your Antiprocrastination Plan" worksheet with this practice exercise at http://www.newharbinger.com/52434. Some examples include:

- Returning to the task after a break

- Handling interruptions

- Managing the effects of ADHD, such as getting distracted

Your antiprocrastination plan might have ramifications in your interpersonal/social worlds. Adults with ADHD often notice that they're better at follow-through on plans that include or affect others, such as study partners. The next section focuses on the social aspect of planning and follow-through.

Interpersonal Domain: How Does Your Procrastination Affect Others?

Often, you're in a one-on-one standoff between your plan and procrastination. No one else is privy to how it turns out. Yet, antiprocrastination isn't a solitary issue when what you do or don't do affects others.

In fact, working with and around others can promote follow-through. Recruiting a body double or an accountability partner to team up with on a task, such as a study partner, helps both parties adhere to plans. Some adults with ADHD find it helpful to work in a library, a coffee shop, or another venue away from at-home distractions where the presence of others provides cues to stay on task.

Your task valuation can include its relevance for your relationships. You might motivate yourself to work on a task by considering your accountability to others, such as a workgroup. You also might be driven to complete a project before a weekend getaway with your partner. Some adults with ADHD use social media for accountability, posting plans—"time to wash my car"—and outcomes later.

=========================== **Practice** ===========================

These questions help you consider any social effects of your task plan. You can download the "Stay Motivated with Your Antiprocrastination Plan" worksheet with these questions at http://www.newharbinger.com/52434.

How is this task relevant to my social world?

_____

_____

_____

How might this task benefit relationships at work? School? Family/personal life?

_____

_____

_____

What relationships inform my task valuation that could help motivate me?

_____

_____

_____

Are there body doubles, social settings, or help from others that will support my task plan?

_____

_____

_____

How would I support a friend who faced this same situation?

_____

_____

_____

Self-compassion is a relationship domain skill because it involves tending to your relationship with yourself. It's an important skill to help you bounce back from invariable slipups in procrastination.

The antiprocrastination plan and other skills in this workbook are designed to help you make informed decisions about how you spend yourself. Not all nonpriority or off-task activity is procrastination. You have a daily planner and to-do lists so that you can rework plans when needed due to factors outside your control.

Practice

Use this exercise to deal with potential barriers to your antiprocrastination plan. At the same time you're fending off escape-avoidance, you can build up your intentions, abilities, and self-trust. You can download the "Stay Motivated with Your Antiprocrastination Plan" worksheet with these questions at http://www.newharbinger.com/52434.

Cognitive Domain

How am I thinking about my task plan?

_____

_____

_____

How might my thoughts be distorted or underestimate my abilities, my "enough-ness"?

_____

_____

_____

Can I tolerate and invest some discomfort to get started?

_____

_____

_____

What is the worst case for my task plan? Best case? Most likely case?

_____

_____

_____

What is a more helpful mindset for facing this task and its value to me?

_____

_____

_____

Behavioral Domain

What are my typical escape behaviors? Digital distractions? Procrastivity tasks?

_____

_____

_____

How can I remove or handle temptations and distractions? Can I tolerate them?

_____

_____

_____

What are the action steps in my task plan that will most help me get engaged?

_____

_____

_____

How good will my "future self" feel when I follow my plan?

_____

_____

_____

Emotional Domain

What am I feeling right now about my task plan?

_____

_____

_____

What emotion words describe my feelings?

_____

_____

_____

Is there a personalized label I could give my feelings?

_____

_____

_____

What are the bodily sensations associated with my emotions?

_____

_____

_____

What information are these emotions giving me? Is there a theme with these emotions?

_____

_____

_____

Implementation Domain

What are useful "If/When *X*, then *Y*" implementation statements that can help me avoid procrastination? (These might cover what *not* to do.)

_____

_____

_____

_____

_____

_____

Interpersonal Domain

How is this task relevant to my social world?

_____

_____

_____

How might this task benefit relationships at work? School? Family/personal life?

_____

_____

_____

What relationships inform my task valuation that could motivate me?

_____

_____

_____

Are there body doubles, social settings, or help from others that will support my task plan?

_____

_____

_____

How would I support a friend who faced this same situation?

_____

_____

_____

Remember, you don't have to feel totally inspired to initiate your plan. Do imagine the relief and satisfaction you'll feel from accomplishing it.

Summary

Procrastination is likely the most common and corrosive issue faced by adults with ADHD. It undoes your intentions and thereby your goals. What's so insidious about procrastination is that it's very personal. You chose your goals and endeavors. They are important to you in some way. They are connected to your sense of self.

Procrastination and time management are also relevant to your relationships. The interpersonal domain of the adult ADHD–anxiety connection is the focus of chapters 6 and 7. Chapter 6 builds on skills from previous chapters to help you see how ADHD affects relationships and how you want to be in relationships. It also covers how to nurture healthy connections with others. Chapter 7 focuses on using skills to manage rejection sensitivity and other stressful relationship circumstances.

CHAPTER 6

Social Capital in Your Social Life and Relationships

Did you ever zone out in class and get called on by the teacher with no clue what was going on? What about making a promise to someone close to you, but then you totally flaked and forgot it? What about being the last one to board a plane or to pick up your child from daycare and you get "the look"?

These examples illustrate the public-facing vulnerabilities experienced by people with ADHD. Many snafus occur in private, but far too many ADHD-related missteps are on vivid display. They can affect others and potentially your relationships with them. You may distinctly recall the classmates giggling at your "Huh, what?" when a teacher's question yanked you out of a daydream. Maybe you've seen frustrated eye rolls from bosses and your partner. Some people, while trying to be encouraging, insert a big "but." Statements may include: "You do great work, *but* it's always late." "I value our friendship, *but* your lateness is disrespectful." "I love you, *but* I don't want to hear that ADHD is your excuse."

This chapter focuses on adult ADHD coping skills for navigating your social worlds. Using the SAP plan of specific, actionable plans at targeted pivot points, the first few sections will address the broad, vague, nonspecific task of managing relationships. We'll define *social capital* and describe the concept of accounts in relationships. We'll talk about how you can use social capital as a framework to understand relationships and the specific roles you play. Next you'll apply emotion-regulation skills to social emotions and their themes. As with other feelings, especially anxieties and sensitivities in social situations, you can decipher signals and meanings. From this foundation, you'll apply specific, actionable strategies for managing relationships. This includes self-compassion, which is how you relate to yourself.

What Is Social Capital?

Social capital is a financial analogy that views relationships as akin to joint savings accounts you open with others (Ramsay 2020). Your connection, this account with someone, comprises a series of deposits and withdrawals with one another. This reflects the give-and-take expectations of different relationships. The idea of capital—shared assets—provides a framework to make sense of mutual expectations in various social domains and different types of relationships, each with different rules and trade-offs. The social capital analogy is a way to track and assess your standing with others and sustain, reconcile, or, in some cases, close these accounts, all of which are issues for adults with ADHD.

Most relationships involve trade-offs where two (or more) people work together and contribute to getting some benefit out of the connection. These connections require a healthy give-and-take, so that everybody benefits and is invested in sustaining the bond (the account). ADHD can make it hard to tune into and track relationship demands and the needs of others while still making sure your needs are met—both necessary skills. The grim reality, though, is that your social sense must be tuned to notice if someone doesn't play fair, isn't trustworthy, or might be toxic. Emotions play an important role in this social sense.

Within the emotional domain, you have social emotions. *Social emotions* can be thought of as the social glue for tracking and reconciling your social capital accounts. For example, if you arrived glaringly late for a work meeting, you probably felt embarrassed. This feeling signified that you didn't fulfill an expectation to be on time. That same feeling can motivate you to balance your account and arrive early next time. Conversely, praise from your boss is a deposit into your shared social capital account. The resulting pride and sense of accomplishment that you feel can motivate you to continue to do good work.

Social emotions are very influential and can be powerful. This is great when things are going well, and your accounts are balanced. But these feelings can be daunting when things aren't going well, or you perceive that they're not. What's more, relationships at work or school are different from those with friends, family, and loved ones. These different relationship groupings come with different expectations, standards, and rules. For example, you may guard against being too informal at work and try to avoid being bossy at home.

Different Relationship Groups

Because you face different coping challenges in your professional life and your personal life, it's helpful to adapt your ADHD coping skills accordingly. Haidt (2006) suggested two social vectors: the *belongingness* vector of your personal relationships and the *status* vector of work, school, or other performance-based settings.

The *belongingness* vector is composed of those bonds from which you draw your sense of personal connection and support. These are your friendly, familial, and affectionate connections. This group includes family members, romantic partners, friends, and others you may not know well but have a passing familiarity with, such as neighbors.

The belongingness vector focuses on relationships with accounts that have established a degree of give-and-take. You assume that people in these relationships will be honest and reliable and deal in good faith with you. There's an expectation of *reciprocal altruism*—"I'll scratch your back, and you'll scratch mine." There may be unconditional positive regard for each other. In the closest relationships, such as with parents, there may be loan forgiveness.

The *status* vector comprises work, school, or other settings and roles that have performance or productivity expectations. Examples include a student or teacher in a class, an employee or boss, or a member of a volunteer organization. The status vector focuses on a *social hierarchy,* your reputation or standing with others. The idea of a hierarchy can sound cutthroat, for example, feeling like you failed if you're not at the top. The broader perspective, though, is that of fulfilling your appointed role.

Role fulfillment along the status vector might be as simple as showing up on time and doing your job, or as complex as organizing and managing others to sustain a business. There are many ways to maintain a good reputation. For example a hard-to-deal-with person who is an expert in their discipline and a person whose work is uneven but who's a team player both satisfy needs and roles within a group.

The following table further details characteristics of the status vector's social hierarchies and the belongingness social vector's reciprocal altruism.

Characteristics of Social Vectors

Status Vector Social Hierarchies	Belongingness Vector Reciprocal Altruism
Social reputation	Personal connection
Organizational performance norms	Social norms in group context (for example, in a family)
Organizational social/political norms	Loyalty
Hierarchy/pecking order	Honesty
Professional relationships, such as peers, colleagues, or mentor-mentee	Reciprocity
Bureaucracy	Reliability
Coordination, alliances	Good-faith coordination, tit-for-tat
Trade-offs, nonzero sum (win-win)	Communication (verbal and nonverbal)
Communication (verbal and nonverbal)	Amends, acceptance, unconditional positive regard
	Coregulation

Reflection

Reflect on your relationships and social capital accounts. Think about stresses where improved coping skills could help. Also note your relationship accounts that are strong and supportive and make you feel well-connected.

_____   _____

_____   _____

_____   _____

_____   _____

_____   _____

Most of your social snafus are presumably unintentional and symptomatic of ADHD, but your emotional reactions can still be strong. Such reactions include stress and worry about what others might think of you and your standing with them. At other times, you might feel blindsided by others' reactions, having no idea that something was wrong. The next section focuses on these social emotions as part of your workbook journey for tending to your relationships.

Social Emotions and Relationships

Human executive functions evolved due to the survival demands of living in ever-expanding groups of nonrelated humans (Barkley 2012; 2015). The need to work and play well with others increased when cooperation and performance expectations had life-or-death consequences in the struggle for survival.

Situations are not as dramatic now, but relationships are still important. Social emotions still influence alliances, especially with people who are not relatives. They also alert us when people cheat the system or otherwise don't operate in good faith. Thus, our emotional wiring is attuned to reading and dealing with other people in multiple settings and with different roles through emotional self-regulation.

The consistent inconsistency of ADHD likely often gets in the way of managing the demands of your roles and relationships. It also makes it harder to catch all the nuanced social rules and signals. For example, you may have trouble reading others' reactions and moods in social settings or deciphering and effectively managing your emotional reactions to others. These challenges may have shown up in childhood in other group situations, such as managing frustration while waiting for your turn. They may continue into adulthood, such as not seeing when someone else wants to say something or keeping your cool when receiving constructive feedback. Guilt and shame are two commonly cited reactions to the effects of ADHD-related social difficulties. Guilt reflects a feeling of embarrassment that you have done something wrong, such as making a social faux pas. Shame reflects a painful feeling from violating more serious norms or standards (or thinking you have done so), which manifests as humiliation or losing face.

When all is good in relationships, you feel secure and are at your best with others. When things aren't going well and you feel vulnerable around others, you'll be more prone to stress and anxiety. In extreme cases of feeling unsafe, you might shut down and withdraw altogether (Porges 2021). Your social emotions are like account notifications from your bank. Social emotions provide signals about your standing with others. They also guide your sense of morality and conscience in social groups (Wright 1994), for example, guiding you to observe norms within a community. Your communities may include your neighborhood block, an office or classroom, or your household, for instance.

In the same way that anxieties have common themes of risk and uncertainty, social emotions have themes that can help you understand how you perceive interpersonal situations. These perceptions of yourself and others guide understanding of your social capital accounts. Let's take a look at some social emotions and their themes in terms of the social information they provide.

Examples of Social Emotions

Here are examples of positive social emotions and their themes in a social setting:

- *admiration:* seeing something of value that another person offers

- *affection:* feeling an attachment—liking someone and enjoying being with them

- *ambition:* striving to achieve, including status-seeking

- *compassion:* being calmly present with someone in distress

- *empathy:* feeling and showing concern for others

- *gratitude:* feeling gratefulness for favors—this feeling guides reciprocity

- *inspiration:* feeling energized or motivated by the actions of another person

- *love:* feeling deep, enduring affection and regard

- *pride:* enjoying the positive feeling of doing something well

- *triumph:* enjoying a positive achievement, including vanquishing a competitor

Reflection

Circle the positive social emotions listed above that resonate with you. List any other positive social emotions in the status and belongingness vectors of your life.

_____

_____

_____

_____

Let's look at examples of unpleasant social emotions and their themes.

- *disgust:* feeling moral repugnance, repulsion for unseemly actions

- *embarrassment:* feeling awkwardness from committing a frowned-upon social act (or even considering such an act)

- *envy:* feeling negative or diminished social comparison with others

- *guilt:* feeling remorse after having made a mistake (or assuming you have)

- *indignation:* feeling righteous anger at someone violating norms or morals that you uphold

- *jealousy:* feeling loss of status or losing out on a particular opportunity

- *resentment:* feeling anger at being mistreated by someone else or a sense of unfairness

- *shame:* feeling of making a moral blunder (or assuming you have), violating norms, losing face

In case you are looking for it, rejection is an event, not a feeling. However, it's an event that will cause you to have hurt feelings called *rejection emotions,* such as sadness, anxiety, and anger (Leary et al. 1998).

Reflection

Circle the unpleasant social emotions listed above that resonate with you. List any other unpleasant social emotions in the status and belongingness vectors of your life.

_____

_____

_____

_____

Dealing with Relationship Slipups

Social emotions, both positive and unpleasant, help promote acts that sustain a relationship or inhibit potentially inappropriate acts. They prompt you to take corrective action and make amends when necessary. For example, if you forgot to answer a friend's lunch invitation, you'll feel a twinge of guilt that spurs a quick my-bad apology and RSVP. Likewise, gratefulness for a friend's favor energizes your expression of thanks and alertness for a chance to repay the favor. These feelings are the social glue that helps maintain tradeoffs in a friendship account that balance out and sustain it in the long run.

Using the social capital analogy broadly is a way to think about your relationships as accounts. This view extends the coping SAP plan of specific, actionable tasks at targeted pivot points to relationships. You can use the SAP plan to promote balanced accounts with others by completing relationship-enriching tasks. In turn, these actions strengthen interpersonal bonds.

The time-management and antiprocrastination exercises you did before may or may not have included examples that involved others in your life. The next practice exercise is an after-the-fact, social emotion debriefing. Its aim is to maintain an adaptive perspective that allows you to manage your feelings, including social-status anxiety over loss of standing with others.

Practice

The following example focuses on the embarrassment of arriving on the wrong day for an appointment. This is something most adults with ADHD have experienced and Trent faced. The responses in the example are his.

Example

Trent arrived at a crowded waiting room of his dentist's office for an appointment and learned he arrived on the wrong day.

Describe the situation and what happened in behavioral terms.

I walked into a crowded waiting room and learned my appointment was for next month, so I was a month early.

What thoughts do you have about the situation?

I can never go back and show my face there! I assume that everyone there is silently laughing at me and judging me, and I'm judging myself.

What do you feel?

I feel embarrassed at such a simple mistake and angry at myself because I used a day off from work for it.

What social emotions do you feel?

Embarrassment, obviously, shame, and disgust with myself. This is my "No one else is as disorganized as I am" frustration.

To what degree does your reaction make sense?

My reaction makes perfect sense because it's clearly my mistake. It's frustrating to be so disorganized.

To what degree is your reaction out of proportion?

It's a fact that I'm a month early. I'm being too hard on myself, though, because I'm the only one inconvenienced. It's better than being a month late, though it's still embarrassing.

What steps will you take to make amends or avoid a repeat, if relevant?

No amends are necessary. I confirmed my actual appointment date, verified that it is in my planner, and signed up for text reminders.

What is an objective way to make sense of the situation and move forward?

Everyone in the waiting room has probably forgotten the situation. I'm not the first person who's done something like this. My embarrassment means I will continue to strive to be organized and reliable, but nobody's perfect.

Your Responses

Now, answer the same questions using your own example. You can download the "Dealing with Relationship Slipups" worksheet with these questions at http://www.newharbinger.com/52434. Working through this exercise will help you reevaluate your automatic reactions and maintain objectivity.

Describe the situation and what happened in behavioral terms.

_____

_____

_____

What thoughts do you have about the situation?

_____

_____

_____

What do you feel?

_____

_____

_____

What social emotions do you feel?

_____

_____

_____

To what degree does your reaction make sense?

_____

_____

_____

To what degree is your reaction out of proportion?

_____

_____

_____

What steps will you take to make amends or avoid a repeat, if relevant?

_____

_____

_____

What is an objective way to make sense of the situation and move forward?

_____

_____

_____

A reframe for keeping mistakes in perspective is to consider the level of offense. Even if you're in the wrong, was your mistake a felony? A misdemeanor? A citation? Was it more like a parking ticket or jaywalking? Try to keep it in perspective.

Even if you see your mistake as egregious, would you judge a friend, especially one with ADHD, as harshly? Many adults with ADHD describe being able to provide good advice and support to others but not themselves. Such perspective-taking is an avenue for self-compassion—soothing and nurturing yourself—which is discussed next.

Self-Compassion

Self-compassion concerns an important relationship—your relationship with yourself. This isn't a me-first, self-centered approach. Rather, it's the idea that you deserve the same regard and charity in the face of imperfection as anyone else. Consider how you'd react to a friend's embarrassment at arriving on the wrong day for an appointment. I'll guess that you'd be supportive, maybe more so than with yourself in that situation. This is why such perspective-taking reframes can be so eye-opening.

Negative self-talk, including self-criticism, is another form unhelpful thoughts take. The internal dialogue elicited by ADHD-caused snafus can be quite harsh and unforgiving. I've heard clients be so self-berating and nasty in their self-judgments that I remark, "If someone else spoke to you like that, they'd be cited for verbal assault." Yes, it's important to be honest with yourself about mistakes and ways to make amends and improve, but this can be achieved in forgiving, forward-looking ways.

A useful self-talk strategy to support self-compassion is distanced self-talk (Kross 2021). *Distanced self-talk* is talking to yourself aloud in the second or third person, the same way you would when speaking to someone else. This means referring to yourself as *you* or by name. I've also had some clients have success using the first-person *we*.

Self-talk using the first person *I* is *immersive self-talk*. When working through emotions with immersive self-talk, you run the risk of getting stuck in unhelpful rumination. Lab-based studies of distanced self-talk have shown it promotes better emotion regulation and task initiation (Kross 2021). It's also an antiprocrastination tool. Distanced self-talk likely draws on your kindness toward others. Verbally describing your feelings and task plans helps you process and work through them.

Writing out feelings and journaling are other helpful distancing strategies. For example, when you're frustrated with someone, you can write a letter that you never send. You can also write a supportive letter to yourself.

Practice

Let's practice distanced self-talk and externalizing feelings through writing. Below are scenarios related to getting started on a task, dealing with emotions, or managing snafus that require self-compassion. Write your responses to them referring to yourself in the third person by name or in the second person as *you*, as you would if you were helping someone else with ADHD. For example, if the situation is "You showed up on the wrong day for your appointment," you might respond by writing, "You'll feel frustrated at first, which is normal, but the feeling will lessen. You can keep the next appointment and handle it with grace and humor if the situation is mentioned."

You must write a report for work (or other writing task, like thank-you notes).

_____

_____

_____

You aren't in the mood to exercise.

_____

_____

_____

The kitchen or your desk is a mess, and you don't know where to start to organize it.

_____

_____

_____

You forgot someone's birthday.

_____

_____

_____

You must tell a boss, teacher, or friend that you'll be late with a promised item.

_____

_____

_____

You lost your credit card. You must cancel it and wait for a new one, which inconveniences the rest of your family.

_____

_____

_____
_____

The purpose of self-compassion is not necessarily to put yourself first all the time. But you need not dismiss yourself or your needs when supporting others. Self-compassion sets a foundation for the underutilized skills of self-advocacy and assertiveness, which are discussed next.

Self-Advocacy and Assertiveness

Assertiveness is one of those skills that sounds great but is hard to do. It can be thought of as the quality of being able to say what you believe or want in a confident, straightforward way. Self-advocacy is a variant of assertiveness. In the context of ADHD, it's typically voiced as the need to ask for help, seek accommodations, and otherwise speak up for resources that allow you to manage ADHD and use your strengths. This can be a particular challenge for college students with ADHD navigating on-campus bureaucracies and services.

Assertiveness is often conflated with aggressiveness—for example, "Don't take no for an answer." It's particularly worrisome for adults with ADHD who are concerned they'll lose even more social capital if their request is rejected or their concerns are dismissed.

Right or wrong, brush-offs can happen. However, most people find that they feel better for having spoken up for themselves, even if the answer is no. Succumbing to discomfort and not speaking up can leave you feeling regret. (_Why didn't I ask when I had the chance?_) More importantly, there's a good chance that things will work out in your favor when you speak up.

The following define-your-role strategy is a behavioral recipe for assertiveness and self-advocacy (Ramsay 2020).

1. Define the situation in specific, actionable terms.

2. Define your role in this situation.

3. Define what you must do to fulfill your role in this situation.

4.   What is a behavioral script or recipe for the action you must perform to fulfill your role? A quick-and-easy reframe for assertiveness is restating facts as you see them. (For example, "I think I ordered French fries with my sandwich, not potato chips.")

5.   Identify and manage any mind-reading thoughts, negative predictions, or other factors out of your control, such as how the other person might react. You can control how you present or say something but not how the other person reacts. (That said, part of step 4 is fashioning a script that increases the likelihood of positive outcomes.)

6.   Anticipate potential barriers to enacting your script, including discomfort, and workarounds.

7.   Implement your plan via your behavioral script. Once you have made your point or made your request, you have fulfilled your role. There may be more discussion or negotiation, but somehow it will be resolved.

This framework makes assertiveness specific and actionable. You can be assertive in a collaborative, even cordial fashion, sharing your viewpoint or request. You then respectfully allow the other person to respond.

Practice

Here is an example of a design-your-own strategy from when Susan struggled with whether to reach out for help with a project. Read Susan's example and then practice with your own example. You can download the "Define-Your-Role Strategy Steps" worksheet with this list of questions at http://www.newharbinger.com/52434.

Example

1.   What is the problem or situation? Phrase in specific, actionable terms.

     I'm behind on a big work project. Some things are still unclear to me, though they made sense before. I need help to make sure I'm on the right track. I'm worried I'll frustrate my boss if I ask for help with something that was already explained.

2.   What is your role in this situation?

     I'm on the project team. My task is unclear. My role is to ask my boss for clarification and guidance to get unstuck and reduce my stress.

3. What must you do to fulfill your role?

   I'll request a meeting with my boss about my portion of the project now, rather than waiting. I'll also ask for weekly check-ins to help me stay on track for the deadline.

4. What is an action plan you can use to fulfill your role?

   To fulfill my role I can say, "I want to meet with you to update you on where I'm at with the project and get your feedback. Moving ahead, it would be helpful for me to have regular check-ins with you to make sure I'm on the right track. Can we do that?"

5. Are you engaging in any mind-reading or negative predictions about things out of your control?

   I'm worried she'll be angry and lose confidence in me. I can't control her reaction. Getting clarity is the right thing to do even if it's difficult. I'll feel unstuck rather than regret holding back.

6. Are there any barriers to follow-through with this plan?

   My boss will be on vacation next week, so I must act soon. This is a reasonable ask, and I'll feel better after it is done.

7. How will you implement your action plan?

   Email is easier, but I'm better face-to-face and can make sure I understand things in real time. When I meet with her, I'll use the script that I wrote out to make my request and let her answer.

8. Summarize the implementation and outcome.

   My boss and I met in the morning before the office got busy. She provided clarification and guidance where I was stuck but said I'm on the right track. She agreed to regular check-ins, which helps.

Your Responses

Now use an example of assertiveness or self-advocacy relevant to you that follows the design-you-own strategy. You can download the "Define-Your-Role Strategy Steps" worksheet with this list of questions at http://www.newharbinger.com/52434.

1. What is the problem or situation? Phrase in specific, actionable terms.

    _____

    _____

    _____

2. What is your role in this situation?

    _____

    _____

    _____

3. What must you do to fulfill your role?

    _____

    _____

    _____

4. What is an action plan you can use to fulfill your role?

    _____

    _____

    _____

5. Are you engaging in any mind-reading or negative predictions about things out of your control?

    _____

    _____

    _____

6. Are there any barriers to follow-through with this plan?

    _____

    _____

    _____

7. How will you implement your action plan?

_____

_____

_____

8. Summarize the implementation and outcome.

_____

_____

_____

You can use the define-your-role strategy for almost any matter, but it's especially useful when you're asking for help. However, you must be willing to accept help. Susan often felt guilty asking her boss for follow-up meetings. It's easy to see a request as a one-sided, burdensome relationship account withdrawal. Instead, try to view the request as providing the other person an opportunity to be supportive. Helpers reap dividends, too. It feels good to help other people. Allow the other person to fulfill their role and field your request. If they provide help, an expression of gratitude by you balances the give-and-take transaction.

This view also reframes asking for help as give-and-take. Both parties benefit. Let's look at some other ways to achieve mutual support.

Other Forms of Give-and-Take Support

Another form of quid pro quo support is body doubling, which was introduced as an antiprocrastination skill in chapter 5. Bartering is a form of body doubling. Bartering is a "You help me with mine, I'll help you with yours" arrangement. You help your neighbor organize their garage on one day, and they help you organize your home office the next day. Essentially, body doubling is a partnership of mutual accountability. You might find a buddy in your neighborhood or at work for a daily walk. Simply having a planned meetup with someone can motivate both of you to get there and be engaged. With more people working from home, virtual coworking groups have increased and are another option that benefits the group who participates.

=========== Reflection ===========

What are some situations where body doubling or another form of bartering would work well for you? List some examples along with people who might be good partners.

Body Doubling

_____

_____

_____

Bartering

_____

_____

_____

The define-your-role strategy is also relevant when fielding requests from others, which is an area where you might find yourself overcommitted and overwhelmed. The issue usually comes up if you have a hard time saying no and other boundary issues, which is the focus of the next section.

Saying No and Other Boundary Issues

Difficulty saying no (or impulsively saying yes) is a common problem for adults with ADHD. *Impulsive compliance* (Ramsay and Rostain 2015a) is a reflex to agree to exciting invitations, projects, or requests but later realizing you can't keep up with existing responsibilities, much less something new. The solution isn't to decline all requests, but first to buy time to make informed choices and to set boundaries, if needed..

Buying time is another coping strategy. When someone makes a request that's appealing but requires substantial time and effort, your reflexive, stock response can be something like "Let me think about it and get back to you."

During the delay, you can fashion terms that, if met, will allow you to say yes. For example, if you're asked to coordinate a school fundraiser, you might be flattered to be asked. After that feeling subsides, though, you may grasp the enormity of what you'd have to do. Instead of saying yes to the initial request, you could offer to work at the ticket booth on the day of the fundraiser.

You'll likely face efforts to persuade you to oversee the whole event. However, use the politician ploy and stay on message and robotically (but assertively) repeat the refrain, "Thanks, but no thanks." Such situations are tailor-made for the "If/When X, then Y" strategy: "If I'm asked to do something time-consuming, then I'll say, 'Let me think about it.'"

Another coping option is to rescind an impulsive yes. Most often you can, upon reflection, decline a request. Feelings of guilt and embarrassment may arise, kindled by thoughts that you "should" keep your word and "tough it out." There'll be times when that's what you do, such as repaying a favor you owe someone, even if it's inconvenient. But there also will be times where it makes sense to consider rescinding an offer to do something. You can weigh the tradeoff of keeping your commitment versus gracefully bowing out due to the effects on your well-being.

Here are the steps of a strategy to say no and set a boundary.

- Hear and understand the request.

- Buy time ("Let me think about it and get back to you").

- Factor the time, effort, and energy involved with the request and consider the effects on your existing commitments and well-being as well as your relationship with the requester.

- Consider what terms would allow you to say yes.

- If your answer is no, say so and stay on message.

- Keep open the option to rescind a yes.

The boundary issue is relevant because adults with ADHD are prone to the allure of novel, exciting opportunities. Sometimes, though, you'll face a real or perceived social capital deficit or debt—the sense that you owe it to someone to say yes. Hence, you say yes to build relationship capital or, more often, to pay down social debt. This pattern is a setup for overpromising and underdelivering, a self-defeating cycle. If you get caught up in this cycle, you run the risk of worsening your relationship status, which the next section discusses.

Social Capital, ADHD Tax, and ADHD Penalties

The ADHD tax refers to the financial costs associated with ADHD. Examples include late fees for overdue bills, parking tickets from forgetfulness, and impulsive purchases. Other financial matters for adults with ADHD include greater debt and less money in savings and retirement accounts (Barkley 2015).

There is a corresponding time tax, along with increased stress, when you deal with the hassle of overdue bills, tickets, and similar financial costs. There's also lost time and emotional and cognitive load costs that go with looking for misplaced stuff, such as cell phones and keys. The ADHD tax also can exact a stress toll on relationships because financial matters, misplaced items, forgotten promises, lateness, and other slipups create strain when they affect other people.

Reflection

List examples of ADHD taxes you pay.

_____   _____

_____   _____

_____   _____

Another type of ADHD penalty, though, can be self-imposed, akin to an expensive service charge (Ramsay 2020). This happens when you sacrifice your self-care or downtime due to falling short of your ambitions. For example: *I can't justify meeting up with friends because I got no household chores done* or *I must skip yoga to catch up on the work I didn't get done at the office.* It's almost like putting yourself in grown-up time-out or grounding yourself.

Yes, there are times when such concessions are necessary, such as meeting an important deadline. Most often, though, this type of penalty is a self-generated, self-defeating punishment. This penalty doubles down on ADHD-related inefficiency by depriving yourself of restorative, self-care activities. It's like ADHD is a loan shark charging outrageous, compounding interest. Follow-through on responsibilities is important, as is rebounding from slipups. Additionally, self-care, such as socializing and exercise, is an essential task. Self-care today is a first step toward coping better tomorrow.

Such self-care is a basic need and a right, not something to be earned, which we will discuss in detail in chapter 8.

A variation of a self-imposed ADHD penalty is self-handicapping. This stems from the guilt and shame adults with ADHD often describe when they presume that they've disappointed others and are indebted to them. For example, a college student granted an assignment extension struggles to meet the new deadline, convinced *My paper has to be one week better than everyone else's*. This was not a condition of the extension but signals the student's guilt, the thought they shouldn't need or don't deserve the extra time.

Overpromising and underdelivering is a manifestation of the self-handicapping ADHD penalty. Like Trent, you may have supposed that your ADHD has created relationship debts that you can't repay, a social capital debtor's prison. You may look back on lateness, forgetfulness, and other examples and wonder how and why your boss, friends, or partner put up with you.

Consequently, when you have a chance to make up for a mistake or pay down your presumed debt with someone, you overpromise: "I'll have the project to you first thing tomorrow," or "I'll have the whole house cleaned by the time you get back." You're well-intentioned, but you've created a new potential letdown or debt of the sort you were trying to undo in the first place. Instead, aim to underpromise and potentially overdeliver, but at least deliver, which is usually a sufficient relationship deposit.

Reflection

Can you recall situations in which you overpromised something, even if your stated commitment was well-intentioned?

_____

_____

_____

What are some situations where you can practice underpromising to set yourself up for success in relationships? What would your underpromising look like?

_____

_____

_____

No doubt, ADHD has real, sometimes detrimental, and potentially ruinous effects on some relationships. Be on guard for your likely tendency to sour cherry–pick your snafus, such as remembering and magnifying mistakes (the negative-filter distortion) and assuming that others are as harsh on you as you are on yourself. Mind-reading others' thoughts and intents are likely the most common relationship distortion. A way to use your ADHD coping skills is to treat your relationships as if they were made up of many role-specific tasks. SAP plans for your social capital can help you make deposits and sustain relationships, which the next section discusses.

Relationships as Tasks

As stated earlier, ADHD is a performance problem, not a knowledge problem. This holds true in relationships. Tending to and improving relationships is a broad, vague, nonspecific goal. Let's look at how you can apply the SAP plan, with its specific and actionable tasks at targeted pivot points, to relationships.

=== Reflection ===

What are common features of ADHD that affect your relationships? Some of these might show up in the belongingness relationship domain but not the status relationship domain, or the converse. Some may show up in both. Circle or comment on the ones relevant to you.

- Disorganization, messiness, clutter, tendency to misplace items

- Strong tendency to start but not finish tasks, take too long, rush at the last minute

- Forgetfulness for recurring household chores, work duties, or important commitments

- Distraction during conversations, poor listening skills

- Emotional reactivity, argumentativeness, defensiveness, poor temper

- Inconsistent follow-though on promises

- Poor sleep habits, difficulties getting started in the morning or staying up too late

- Difficulties coordinating and cooperating with others

- Addictions, such as excessive technology use or gaming

- Deceit, lies to cover up mistakes

- Lateness, poor on-time arrival, absences, last-minute backouts

- Poor job performance

- Lateness with work or homework submissions

- Conflicts at work, viewed as not pulling your share

- Viewed as not adequately contributing to household income, not paying household expenses on time

- Viewed as not adequately contributing to running the household or family

- Reckless driving habits, driving too fast

- Difficulties relaxing or enjoying quiet activities with others

Note any additional common features of ADHD that affect your relationships.

_____

_____

_____

_____

_____

Practice

Let's look at specific, actionable steps and targeted pivot points that can help you improve relationship behaviors. Following are examples to get you started.

- Choose a specific meeting with a person where you will show up early and put a note in your planner.

- Use your commute on public transportation in the morning to respond to texts and emails.

- Make an appointment with yourself and put it in your planner to proactively text or check in with friends.

- With your spouse/partner/roommates, set up a regular check-in day and time (such as Sunday at 6 p.m.) when you can coordinate schedules or talk about other household matters.

- Ask your spouse/partner/child about their day when you come home from work.

- Ask one coworker on Monday about their life outside of work.

- Say good morning to everyone in your workgroup each workday.

- Set up a time to watch a movie with a friend or family member that they like even if you're not interested in it.

- If you live with someone, do something that's meaningful for them, even if you don't think it's a big deal, like hanging up your jacket rather than draping it over a chair when you get home from work.

- Put down your phone when someone talks to you so you can focus on listening.

Name at least one specific, actionable step and targeted pivot point you can implement that will improve at least one relationship behavior. Consider putting it on a to-do list or in your planner if it's recurring, such as taking out the recycling.

_____

_____

_____

_____

Like any habit, relationship tasks are not one-off affairs. Hopefully, some of your relationship skills and tasks become habits. Good coping, especially in relationship accounts, is the ability to rebound from slipups and reestablish consistent use of skills and routines. It's amazing how far a few kindhearted acts and role-fulfilling tasks go in helping get and stay on good terms in relationships.

Summary

This chapter illustrated the importance of executive-function coping in social domains. The social capital analogy of relationships as accounts you share with others is a way to track your standing with others. Also consider framing relationships as tasks for fulfilling your roles and tending to these relationships. Social emotions help us strike a balance in our relationship accounts.

However, you may feel particularly vulnerable to being misunderstood due to ADHD. Your actions or inactions may be misinterpreted as lack of caring. You will likely be criticized for classic ADHD mistakes. Like many adults with ADHD, you might experience trouble with extreme emotional reactions to criticisms and potential rejection. Another issue may be missing important signals and social cues, which can make conversations stressful. In rarer cases, some adults with ADHD find themselves in toxic, even abusive relationships. Chapter 7 explores these topics in more detail.

CHAPTER 7

Coping with Stressful Relationships

Despite your use of the coping skills outlined in chapter 6, like advocating for yourself and taking relationship-building steps, you'll periodically contend with ADHD-related embarrassments, hurt feelings, and others' disappointments. You may even face hurtful teasing or put-downs. You might remember similar feelings growing up and dealing with teachers, parents, and peers who didn't understand or recognize your ADHD. Chapter 7 focuses on some of the more frustrating, often painful experiences endured by adults with ADHD in relationships and social settings. We'll explore skills that will help you better face and get through these painful experiences. Let's start with a biggie for many adults with ADHD: rejection.

Rejection Sensitivity

Do you find yourself overreacting to what you later see as trivial matters, such as ribbing about your misplaced keys? What about feeling like you don't size up well compared to those around you, such as your uber-organized cubicle workmate? Do you have a successful relative who is quick to offer you unhelpful advice—such as "You need to stop procrastinating." Does a boss's comment about your lateness in front of a roomful of colleagues keep running through your mind? Have you reacted by snapping back in anger, breaking into tears, or unleashing a volcanic string of expletives during your car ride home alone after such encounters? These are examples of what is known as rejection sensitivity.

Rejective sensitive dysphoria or *rejection sensitivity* (RS) and its relation to ADHD is a hot topic in ADHD treatment (Dodson 2023). The increasing interest in RS mirrors a growing awareness of the role of emotions in the lives of people with ADHD, especially how emotions connect to relationship stress.

If you're like most adults with ADHD, you've had more than your share of rejections and other frustrations. You've likely faced bothersome labels or misattributions of your difficulties, such as being lazy, unmotivated, insensitive, and unreliable. RS is a once-bitten, twice-shy defense for adults with ADHD that is maybe more like an often-bitten, forever-vulnerable defense. An impaired ability to regulate emotions, a core feature of ADHD (Barkley 2015), magnifies rejection experiences. This inability makes it more difficult to self-soothe and get over rejections.

Studies of distorted thoughts in adults with ADHD have found that the interplay of the experiences of living with ADHD result in frustrations and feelings of depression. These feelings lead to escape-avoidance coping, in turn creating more problems or perceived failures. This cycle becomes a vicious, downward spiral (Knouse, Zvorsky, and Safren 2013). Such unhelpful thoughts and emotional reactions are molded from real experiences and serve a self-protective function by sidestepping potential frustrations. Escape-avoidance, although maladaptive, provides a quick and easy escape hatch.

Even though these mindsets make sense, they're unhelpful because they knock you off track from your goals and chip away at your relationships. You may overgeneralize these thoughts, like a small drop of ink clouding a full glass of water. Consequently, your RS emotions and avoidance interfere with your here-and-now coping, undermining self-trust for your endeavors, especially those affecting your relationships.

Medications approved for ADHD can improve emotion regulation (Surman and Walsh 2022). However, with the overlap of RS and the adult ADHD–anxiety connection, coping strategies can help, too.

Identify RS Triggers

When coping with the overlap of RS and the adult ADHD–anxiety connection, the first step is to identify specific RS triggers. Dodson (2023) wrote that RS is "triggered by the perception that a person has been rejected or criticized… [I]t may also be triggered by a sense of falling short—failing to meet their own high standards or others' expectations." Hence, you might feel heightened sensitivity to others' reactions and your internal criticisms of your performance. This is the relationship version of the ADHD performance anxiety introduced in chapter 2. What's more, social status anxiety is a human factory setting for tracking reputation or social standing (Wright 1994). Still, RS is ADHD-informed social status anxiety magnified by the public-facing frustrations of adult ADHD.

Let's consider some common triggers for RS. "Perfectionism" was by far the most endorsed cognitive distortion for adults with ADHD in a study by our group (Strohmeier et al. 2016). The next two most endorsed were "emotional reasoning and decision-making" and "comparison to others." I'm going beyond the study data here, but you can view perfectionism as linked to emotions involved in making decisions and drawing social comparisons. Perfectionism becomes a means to avoid rejection—for example, *If I'm perfect, I'm safe.*

Experiencing that you're not perfect leaves you vulnerable to potential hurt and rejection. A history of frustrated choices and outcomes may leave you distrustful of yourself and prone to compare yourself negatively to others. You may think about all the ways you don't size up in the ways the world seems to demand. This pattern may lead you to discount your strengths in the face of ADHD-related coping difficulties and assume that others will be fault-finding and critical. Taken together, this process is a recipe for ADHD RS.

Reflection

Let's consider some of the common situations that may trigger RS and anxiety due to ADHD.

- Having a family member, spouse, or coworker point out something you forgot to do

- Having a difference of opinion with someone

- Having someone cut in line in front of you (or someone else point out that you must move to the back of a line)

- Feeling presumably good-natured humor hitting a sore spot

- Worrying that others talk about you behind your back (and not about how great you are)

- Assuming you are working at a deficit or in debt in relationships

- Having excessive concern about how your social media posts come across (or by lack of responses)

- Making negative comparisons with others' social media posts

- Repeatedly scrutinizing relationships and seeing things as all good or all bad, with your mood changing accordingly

- Seeing someone else getting a compliment and it feeling like a loss for you, that maybe you don't size up

List any other examples of triggers that may make you more prone to RS and anxiety due to ADHD.

_____

_____

_____

_____
_____

Research on rejection events not specific to ADHD revealed the following six common categories (Leary et al. 1998). Consider if any of these are relevant to you. (_Disassociation_ in this study refers to ending a personal relationship.)

- criticism

- betrayal

- active disassociation (such as being dumped in a dating relationship)

- passive disassociation (such as no longer being included in a group text or being ghosted)

- being unappreciated

- being teased

List any other examples of rejection events.

_____

_____

_____

These reflections lay a groundwork for grasping the role of your emotions and RS in your relationships. Emotions provide relationship signals, like social status worries or assurances. Social emotions similarly help you take stock of your standing with others. Perceptions and thoughts, which draw on your social history shaped by ADHD, also color your responses to situations. The CBT skills we've discussed so far have been used to help you more consistently turn intentions into actions, which helps in relationships. Other skills for navigating and fostering relationships, such as practicing self-advocacy and maintaining your sense of enough-ness, help you look out for yourself and avoid falling into less-than patterns. Let's bring these skills to bear on your social life and dealing with RS.

Overcoming Your RS Triggers

As basic as it might seem by this point, recognizing that your RS has been triggered is an important first step. This allows you to start using your coping skills, such as adaptive emotional distancing and perspective building sooner and more effectively. You essentially turn down the dial on the magnitude of your RS. This can include situations where you've been rejected or are called out on a mistake and also times when you magnify or misperceive such matters. Let's have you start practicing.

Practice

Example

Read the following example responses and then do the exercise using a personal example.

What situation triggered your RS? Define in behavioral versus emotional terms.

My boss returned my monthly report to me with a message that I must revise it and resubmit it, which has never happened before.

What are your thoughts about this situation?

My boss thought I did a lousy job. My work was unprofessional and makes me look bad.

How can you reevaluate your thoughts?

On second look, many sections had no edits. My boss added a note in one section that what I wrote was fine, but the edits reflect their "style." A colleague shared that they had to resubmit their report, too.

What are your feelings about this situation?

I almost had a panic attack when I first saw it. I was embarrassed and worried I had failed. I was angry at my boss because I worked hard on the report, and the edits seemed nitpicky.

What are your feelings telling you? How can you manage them?

These feelings reminded me of school where I earned bad grades, and teachers said that I needed to work harder. This was despite taking longer than everyone else to complete my work. Now is a chance to have tougher skin and take the edits at face value. I can make the changes and be done with it.

What are you doing or not doing to handle this situation?

I felt better facing it once I started on the changes. I want to accept constructive feedback rather than take it personally, but it's hard. At first, I avoided the rewrites by doing other work and even looked for other jobs.

What is your implementation plan for this situation?

I decided "If I read the first edit, then I'll make changes one at a time."

How do you wield your social capital in this situation?

The report affects my relationship with my boss and my job. I used social capital to check in with my coworker, which helped. I practiced self-compassion. I know that my emotions reflect my desire to do well, but I jump to conclusions that my boss doesn't like me.

Your Responses

Now it's your chance to practice with your own example. Remember that you are trying to turn the dial down on the magnitude of your reactions. You will still have feelings about situations.

What situation triggered your RS? Define in behavioral versus emotional terms.

_____

_____

_____

What are your thoughts about this situation?

_____

_____

_____

How can you reevaluate your thoughts?

_____

_____

_____

What are your feelings about this situation?

_____

_____

_____

What are your feelings telling you, and how can you manage them?

_____

_____

_____

What are you doing or not doing to handle this situation?

_____

_____

_____

What is your implementation plan for this situation?

_____

_____

_____

How do you wield your social capital in this situation?

_____

_____

_____

You will encounter many rejection events throughout life, such as not being selected for a team, having relationships break up, or drifting away from friends. These events will trigger strong feelings but are part of life. Remember that normal, low-level frustrations tied to ADHD can occur within generally stable, reasonably balanced relationships, such as periodic ups and downs with friends or coworkers.

Sadly, there may be social capital accounts that are massively overdrawn by another person. You may see a pattern that suggests it's time to freeze an account or maybe close it altogether due to lack of reciprocity. Keep in mind that just as adults with ADHD tend to overestimate their withdrawals and underestimate their deposits, you might give someone too much debt forgiveness. Trust yourself on whether a relationship provides adequate respect, understanding, and reciprocity. The next section, though, focuses on especially disturbing relationships.

Despite your efforts, some relationships will not work out. It's normal to drift apart from people or have fallings-out, on occasion. In rare cases, you may find yourself engulfed in a toxic relationship that mires you in stress and anxiety. Such toxic relationships might occur when someone attempts to exploit and take advantage of you. We'll review these kind of relationships next so you can be on the lookout.

Bullying and Gaslighting

Many adults with ADHD report a history of being bullied, usually when they were younger. Adult bullying can manifest as coercion, manipulation, and belittlement. Teen girls and young adult women with ADHD are especially at risk for abusive dating and romantic relationships (Hinshaw et al. 2022). Such abuse may reach the level of gaslighting, which can arise in either the belongingness or status domains (see Sarkis 2018; 2022).

Gaslighting is when a predatory schemer deviously and systematically deludes an unwitting target to doubt their perceptions of reality. They do this by casting doubts on the person's memory for and accounts of facts and by dismissing that person's feelings, needs, and ideas. Gaslighters contrive adversities and ascribe negative traits to their target. These supposed adversities and negative traits are used to blame the person for any undesirable happenings. This includes the "you made me do it" justifications for maltreatment. Gaslighting can manifest in work or other settings as harassment, such as blame for things that are not your fault or fabricated poor work ratings. The gaslighter may take credit for your good work. Such tactics are sprinkled with affection, reassurances, and other token gestures that further stoke the target's confusion and self-doubt. Isolating the target from friends and loved ones helps sustain the ruse.

Motivations for such exploitation might be financial control, emotional control within a relationship, or a desire for possessions. In fact, the gaslighter will treat the target as a possession. Targeted people question their worth, including as a viable partner for anyone else. This keeps them enmeshed in the relationship and subjugated.

In some ways, the mistrust theme and consistent inconsistency that define ADHD already infuse such doubts into the minds of many adults with ADHD, akin to self-gaslighting. Such factors are why self-compassion and self-advocacy are important skills to practice.

A recentering point when facing gaslighting is self-trust of what you know to be true and what you know to be false. Gaslighters rely on outwardly persuasive claims that prey on your vulnerabilities. They'll threaten you with the loss of friends, jobs, or money if you don't listen to them. They will couch the warnings in empty promises and sweet talk in an effort to keep you hooked. Such gestures don't constitute real change. Focus on their actions, not their words. Reach out to friends, family, trusted peers, and others who'll provide support and perspective.

The emotional blackmail in gaslighting is one form of relationship abuse. Let's look more at the components of abusive relationships.

Components of Abusive Relationships

Abusive relationships can involve any unwanted physical acts. They can also involve persistent emotional abuse. Emotional abuse often takes the form of verbal abuse, including insults, name-calling, blaming, and threats. Emotional abuse leaves the target on the defensive, dreading their circumstances but feeling trapped (*I don't want to stay, but I can't leave*). Gaslighting-like coercions may signal abuse. For example, key relationship details are kept off-limits like financial decisions and access to funds. The gaslighter may prohibit whom the target can see and what they're allowed to do.

Your safety is of the utmost importance. If you suspect that you are in an abusive relationship, seek professional help, including legal help, to learn your rights and options. If your abuser denies the abuse or is unwilling to change, consider a separation, move out if you live together, and seek out other ways to ensure your safety and well-being (see Sarkis 2020).

Troubled relationships without the abuses described above are still stressful, unsatisfying, and unhealthy. The next section will discuss some common difficulties in ADHD-affected relationships.

Troubled Relationships

Many ADHD-affected couples struggle with poor communication, money and parenting stresses, and other disagreements that can weaken bonds. At least one partner having ADHD makes these typical couple issues worse. Surveys of ADHD-affected couples reveal stressors from common diagnostic features of ADHD (Pera and Robin 2016). The most-cited stressors stem from distractibility, poor memory for details, and poor follow-through on promises. The consistent inconsistency of ADHD undermines role fulfillment expectations for committed relationships and household management. The issues only get more complicated when juggling the demands of work, parenting, finances, and other obligations.

Household chores are a common relationship stress point. For example, early in the relationship, one partner may have simply started doing a chore by default, but this original, unspoken arrangement no longer works. Chores can be renegotiated as circumstances change. Chores can be split up based on what's the best fit for each partner. The same can be done within an office workgroup.

There are other frustrations more specific to a partner with ADHD. Adults with ADHD describe misattributions about intent of their actions or inactions if the other partner doesn't understand ADHD. These are of the "If you loved me, you would (or would not) do X" variety. This doesn't not mean partners with ADHD always get a pass. There's a healthy middle ground where there is mutual understanding of the challenges of ADHD and reasonable discussions and compromises, such as in the chores example above.

Partners without ADHD often benefit from education about the effects of ADHD on relationships. Similarly, partners with ADHD can benefit from effective medical and nonmedical treatments. This includes coping strategies that improve social capital, like a shared household calendar, that are essential for adults with ADHD (Orlov 2010; Pera 2008). The positive results of effective treatment spill over into relationships. For example, better time management, decreased procrastination, and increased follow-through on tasks will have immediate payoffs within relationships at home and at work.

Apart from skills for dealing with RS and avoiding toxic relationships, you can use proactive coping to look out for yourself and be your best self in relationships. This promotes connections that are mutually fulfilling and celebrate your strengths. The next section focuses on strategies to help you create more consistency for yourself along with benefits for your relationships.

Using Coping Skills in Relationships

The effects of ADHD are ever present as you shoulder the demands of your different roles. Your various relationships in your belongingness and status domains can be broken down into a series of role-fulfilling tasks you perform with the aid of your coping skills. We're back to the SAP plan of specific, actionable plans executed at targeted pivot points. It's your go-to reframe for coping in relationships, which also reduces stress and anxiety. Let's look at some of these circumstances and ways to manage them.

Social Rules and Norms

There are signposts in life that provide clear guidance, like enter and exit signs for parking lots. Social norms or rules are not so clear. They're often unspoken, but provide guidance, nonetheless.

On the status dimension, such as work or school, simply asking about the rules for an office or a class, such as "Can I work remotely?" or "Is attendance taken?" is a good use of self-advocacy. This happens in the belongingness domain, too, with questions about what others will wear to an event or how to split a dinner check. There may be some explicit rules, like expected work attire. Simply asking is a good way to ferret out rules or at least discover whether they're hard and fast or not. Other social norms may require you to observe and figure them out. Be on the lookout, but asking still might work.

Some unspoken, unwritten social norms guide one-on-one interactions. A study of criticisms faced by adults with ADHD (Beaton, Sirois, and Milne 2022) showed impulsivity as the main complaint cited in social settings. Examples included interrupting or dominating conversations, saying the wrong thing at the wrong time, and missing other social cues. One way to deal with impulsivity is to know your risky situations and enter them with a plan about what to do or not do. This is yet another way to use the implementation intention skill.

Such social difficulties may come from your yearning to connect with others. If these problems sound familiar, though, having a game plan or behavioral script in advance is useful. For example, in a conversation, you may limit yourself to saying no more than three sentences (Rosenfield, Ramsay, and Rostain 2008). Then pause and give another person a chance to chime in. This adds portion controls to a conversation. Another target is entering business meetings or dinner parties with a plan to hold back from interjecting humorous remarks or other impromptu commentary, at least until you've had a chance to read the room.

These coping ideas draw from the define-your-role strategy for assertiveness that can be repurposed as behavioral scripts for your specific role in social situations. For example, if you tend to overshare personal information or want to ensure you show an interest in others rather than dominating a conversation, develop a plan for the specific situation rather than improvising (*I will ask about them before I mention me*). It's a variant on relationships as tasks, not unlike preparing for a job interview.

Bounded Interactions

You may underutilize your social capital by overlooking your leverage for handling tough situations. Creating bounded or portioned social interactions is a way to manage them more effectively that plays to your strengths and sidesteps weak spots. The longer a social get-together, the greater the cognitive and inhibitory energy needed to sustain your best social self, making it more likely you'll get worn down and succumb to impulses or otherwise lose it.

For example, if a friend invites you for a leisurely dinner, but you know that you'll get restless and distracted after the appetizers, suggest getting together for coffee or a quick lunch. If your family's full-day gathering is sensory overload, plan your arrival and departure for a less stressful, bounded stretch. These are examples of using your capital to arrange for your success. Rather than working harder to sustain attention, make plans that fit your attentional endurance. If your arrow can't hit the target, move the target until it does.

Effective Communication

This topic is like that of assertiveness. It sounds good, but it's hard to do in the heat of a moment. Again, we'll rely on the SAP plan with its specific, actionable plans at targeted pivot points.

Good communication benefits from getting into the right mode or mindset. Scheduled job interviews allow you to walk in prepared with your game face on. Similarly, and especially for discussions in your personal life, scheduling them is better than doing them on the fly.

Schedule meetings or check-ins with a professor, boss, and even your partner about important matters. Such relationship appointments will help you minimize impromptu discussions, where you might be distracted or prone to impulsiveness. Conversations in the belongingness relationship domain about sensitive topics, such as money or parenting, can be touchy. You want to enter that kind of exchange with the goal of being cooperative and open-minded. Coach yourself to keep your emotions in check. For example, fully listen with the aim of understanding, instead of coming up with counterarguments while the other person is talking. Pause and choose your words intentionally when you respond. It's not cheating to arrive with written notes, including tactfully worded, verbatim statements, as well as bullet points you want to cover. You can also take notes during conversations, including those with a partner. Explain that the discussion is important, you value your partner's thoughts, and you want to make sure you understand and remember them.

It's helpful to have an agreed-upon endpoint or other bounding to pace the discussion. It's also useful to agree to cooling-off breaks if feelings become heated. However, cool off with the stipulation that the discussion resumes after a cooldown to reach some sort of fair-minded wrap-up. For committed partners, it's nice to follow the meeting with a bonding activity, like a walk.

Your communication is the part of the equation that you control (your role) and that you can use to set a positive tone for a conversation. One communication skill for advancing a conversation is finding a grain of truth in what the other person says, even if you might disagree with most of it. It's difficult for another person to escalate if you say, "You're right" or "I see where you're coming from." You can augment this agreement with empathic statements that validate the other person's views, such as "I'd feel the same way if I were in your shoes" or "I hear your frustration." These skills allow you to then share your views, using "I feel" statements about behaviors, such as "I feel dismissed when you say you don't want me to mention my ADHD." (See Burns 2020 and Spradlin 2003 for other good tips.)

Such give-and-take approaches help you listen to others, accept their feedback, and enable you to more easily provide feedback and make requests. These communication skills help shape relationships in healthy ways.

Another way you wield influence is choosing the people you surround yourself with. You cannot necessarily control the makeup of your family, workplace, or school, but outside these contexts, you can find supportive people for your social network.

Finding Supportive Groups

A sense of understanding and acceptance is a major source of support in life in general. It is also a protective factor to buffer the effects of criticisms and RS faced by adults with ADHD (Beaton, Sirois, and Milne 2022).

Like asking for and accepting help, finding supportive people requires taking steps to reach out and take advantage of opportunities. To this end, the ADHD community increasingly offers connection opportunities. Many ADHD organizations host virtual meetups, support groups, and speaker events. The Annual International Conference on ADHD offers close contact with experts in ADHD as well as being a get-together for adults with ADHD. The event is cohosted by Children and Adults with Attention-Deficit/Hyperactivity Disorder (CHADD), the Attention Deficit Disorder Association (ADDA), and the ADHD Coaches Organization (ACO). These organizations and their connection opportunities, including through local chapters and programs, are also useful sources of ADHD information for people interested in ADHD, such as loved ones, healthcare professionals, and educators.

Assessing Your Relationship Accounts

Trust your ability to build and tend to your relationships using your skills, including managing them when things get bumpy. Your accounts need not be perfectly balanced. That's okay. There are close relationships in which carrying debt—yours or theirs—is common when there's a good-faith investment history. Others may be imbalanced but not unduly so. However, pay attention to your concerns about the status of the account when you encounter issues such as a lack of reciprocity and support.

I've emphasized ways you can manage relationship tasks that are likely ADHD-related problem areas for you. However, others are also responsible for maintaining accounts with you. Good relationships involve cooperation and compromise. You may have friends who understand how ADHD creates stress for you, such as the friend who accommodates your forgetfulness with kindly text reminders for get-togethers. If you worry that such matters make you seem high maintenance, consider if they're any different than courtesies regarding someone's dietary restrictions. This is the sort of give-and-take that you can look for with others, unapologetically.

Reflection

What are some features of your ADHD that you wish others in your social domains better understood and accommodated?

_____

_____

_____

_____

_____

_____

_____

Summary

Managing relationships is a wide-ranging topic with many nuances because each relationship holds different challenges and opportunities. Although _profiling_ can be a loaded term, we profile our relationships. You know the friend you can trust with a sensitive problem and the one you can't. You also know who understands ADHD and who doesn't even try.

Keep in mind, you are being profiled, too. Humans naturally assess each other's social status. Taking stock in this way helps you select and maintain relationships by having realistic, reciprocal expectations with peers, friends, and loved ones. Adults with ADHD especially benefit from people who value their strengths and understand ADHD.

Chapter 8 highlights your strengths that, combined with your growing skill set, can be harnessed for not only your relationships but also your overall well-being. To this end, we will also review lifestyle issues for further reducing your stress and anxiety.

Manage Stress Using Your Strengths and Self-Care

I hope by this point you are experiencing greater self-trust with your use of the workbook skills. Such successes you might notice include bouncing back from the slipups that everyone faces.

Sometimes, though, CBT for adult ADHD is a downer. You're asked to notice distorted thoughts, executive dysfunction, self-mistrust, the discomfort of anxiety feelings, and work, school, and relationship problems. The list of demands may feel like it goes on and on. Pain points are a necessary starting point to untangle ADHD's role in procrastination, poor time management, relationship struggles, and the layering of stress and anxiety. From this foundation, you can reverse engineer them and make positive changes.

The skills you've gained from this workbook will help you continue to not only turn intentions into actions but also let loose your strengths and aptitudes. These strengths can be used to sustain your progress and revisit earlier interrupted or abandoned goals. Let's now explore health and well-being topics that can help boost your coping efforts to live well with ADHD. Let's start by taking stock of your strengths.

What Are Your Character Strengths?

The *Values in Action Inventory of Strengths* (VIA-IS; Peterson and Seligman 2004) is an outgrowth of positive psychology. *Positive psychology* is psychological science directed at pinpointing the adaptive features of human nature, such as resilience, post-traumatic growth, and flourishing (Seligman and Csikszentmihalyi 2000). The VIA-IS questionnaire is used to catalog a self-assessed character strengths profile. You can easily complete the VIA-IS online for free, but let's use its list of character strengths for a reflection.

Reflection

The VIA-IS categories are described below. Check off your strong suits.

- ☐ *Creativity:* clever, problem-solver, sees things in unique ways

- ☐ *Curiosity:* interested in new things, open to new ideas

- ☐ *Judgement:* critical thinker, open-minded, thorough thinker

- ☐ *Love of learning:* seeks to master new skills and topics, looks to learn

- ☐ *Perspective:* wise, big-picture thinker, provides good advice

- ☐ *Bravery:* valor, speaks up for what's right, doesn't avoid due to fear

- ☐ *Perseverance:* persistence, conscientiousness, finishes what's started

- ☐ *Honesty:* authentic, trustworthy, sincere

- ☐ *Zest:* enthusiastic, energetic, all-in, doesn't do things half-heartedly

- ☐ *Love:* genuine, warm, values close bonds

- ☐ *Kindness:* generous, caring, compassionate, altruistic

- ☐ *Social intelligence:* picks up on others' motives and feelings, knows what makes others tick

- ☐ *Teamwork:* team player, socially responsible, loyal

- ☐ *Fairness:* evenhanded, doesn't let feelings bias decisions about others

- ☐ *Leadership:* organizes group activities, encourages a group's objectives

- ☐ *Forgiveness:* forbearing, accepts others' shortcomings, bestows second chances

- ☐ *Humility:* modest, unpretentious

- ☐ *Prudence:* careful, cautious, doesn't take undue risks

- ☐ *Self-regulation:* self-controlled, manages impulses and emotions

- ☐ *Appreciation of beauty and excellence:* feels awe and wonder in beauty, inspired by others

- ☐ *Gratitude:* thankful for the good, grateful, feels blessed

☐ *Hope:* optimistic, future-minded

☐ *Humor:* playful, elicits smiles, lighthearted

☐ *Spirituality:* seeks meaning, purpose-driven, senses a connection with the sacred

Additional strengths were identified from research interviews with successful adults with ADHD (Sedgwick, Merwood, and Asherson 2019). Check off your strong suits.

☐ *Divergent thinking:* outside-the-box, innovative ideas, flowing thoughts

☐ *Hyperfocus:* targeted, sustained focus, productive state

☐ *Nonconformist:* feeling different, outsider

☐ *Adventurousness:* thrill-seeking, seeking experiences and challenges

☐ *Self-acceptance:* ability to see one's strengths despite difficulties, charitable of others

☐ *Sublimation:* gravitate to strengths, aptitudes, and passions as redirection from difficulties

Let's move from this reflection to an exercise in which you consider how to use your strengths.

Practice

This is a hybrid practice-reflection. Answer the following questions. Consider revisiting these questions periodically.

What are some tasks, endeavors, or goals in your life you want to pursue? What personal strengths and skills in this book can help you achieve some of these?

_____

_____

_____

What are some personal situations that have been affected by the adult ADHD–anxiety connection that you now are empowered to approach differently?

_____

_____

_____

Is there any unfinished business, endeavors, or goals that you'd set aside that you want to revisit?

_____

_____

_____

What are some specific discomforts or anxieties in your daily life that you're now ready to face, including seemingly trivial ones? (Remember: we build up from the small stuff.)

_____

_____

_____

_____

Now that you've identified your character strengths, let's look at ways to use them with your health and well-being.

Taking Care of Yourself

I introduced self-compassion as your relationship with yourself. Indeed, the first executive function to emerge is the recognition that you're a distinct *self* that requires regulation to preserve (Barkley 2015). Self-care is thus essential, and emotions provide a barometer of your bodily needs (Mlodinow 2022). The benefits of self-care help buffer the effects of stress and ADHD and thereby support coping. Let's look at ways you can promote self-care, starting with a foundational need: good sleep.

Sleep

Sleep difficulties are common in adult ADHD. Certain ADHD symptoms contribute to sleep problems, such as difficulties turning off your thoughts, staying up late to catch up on undone tasks, or procrastinating on going to sleep to enjoy some peaceful alone time after the day's stresses. You might fight off sleep, even when you're dog-tired, to stretch out today a little longer to avoid facing tomorrow's stress.

A first step toward better sleep is treating sleep as a task. As in other antiprocrastination plans, start with sleep valuation. Setting a "get into bed to sleep" time gives you a pivot point. Working backward from this target, build a script of steps designed to get you into sleep mode. Include in the script lead-up tasks, like readying clothes and other items for the next day.

Household cues can provide bedtime pivot points. For example, going to bed with your partner can cue you that it's bedtime. You might go to bed after completing a final evening task, such as packing lunch for tomorrow or brushing your teeth.

If you resist sleep because it's boring or tense, comfort media is a compromise. *Comfort media* refers to enjoying videos, podcasts, or books in bed to foster sleep. The essential catch, though, is that you choose content you're very familiar with. You've read, watched, or heard the content many times before and know it well. It's enjoyable, but it's not going to keep you awake, unlike something activating like a page-turner book or political interview. Comfort media is like a child's bedtime story that's soothing and helps put you to sleep.

The "get in bed" pivot point is half the equation. The arguably more important half is keeping your wake-up time the same every day and sticking to it regardless of how you slept or when you went to sleep. More precisely, it's your "wake up and get out of bed" pivot point, the hard start to your day. Such sleep restriction, a central principle in cognitive behavioral treatment for insomnia, is useful for ADHD morning difficulties. Getting up and engaging in your day gives you focus and energy to help you get through it.

Reflection

Think about some things that you can do to wind down your day and get into sleep mode. Here are some examples.

- Select tomorrow's clothes.

- Ready items for work or school, such as a computer bag or backpack.

- Charge gadgets.

- Prepare lunch for tomorrow (yours or your children's).

- Pick up around the house.

- Tend to pets.

- Enjoy pleasure media before bed.

- Practice relaxation or mindfulness exercises.

- Brush your teeth, do a skin-care regimen, or perform other evening routines.

- Use comfort media in bed.

Note other activities that can help you get into sleep mode.

_____

_____

_____

_____

Good sleep supports good routines and better management of ADHD. Good sleep also supports your body's regulatory processes, including appetite and energy, which the related tasks and habits discussed next also support.

Exercise and Healthy Eating

Like doubts you had about using a planner, you might think, *Where will I find time to prepare healthy food and exercise?* This section draws on the SAP plan of specific, actionable tasks with targeted pivot points to promote healthy behaviors, starting with exercise.

EXERCISE

I'm using a broad definition of *exercise* as any sort of movement or activity that contributes to your overall health. There's an activity range from sedentary on one end to vigorous exercise at the other, with a basic objective to reduce sedentary behavior (2018 Physical Activity Guidelines Advisory Committee 2018). If you have established routines, like yoga class or biking, put them in your planner to organize and track them. If you aim to establish an exercise time, use your planner to find open slots before, after, or in between other responsibilities. Exercise is also a job for your antiprocrastination skills for time-bounding (for example, thirty minutes walking on a treadmill) or task-bounding (walk twice around the block).

Exercise is both a have-to and a want-to task. You want the benefits, and you'll feel good afterward. However, it's a hassle that's easy to escape-avoid. It's another case when the precondition to be in the mood is unrealistic. An exercise-focused implementation plan, such as "When I pick up my car keys, then I'll go to yoga class" or "If I put on my sneakers, then I'll walk around the block" helps. Body doubling, for example, with a walking partner, improves follow-through.

Exercise provides short-term benefits for ADHD symptoms (Ratey 2008) apart from other known benefits. Exercise reduces stress and can function as a keystone habit (Duhigg 2012). A *keystone* habit is one with positive ripple effects, such as exercise often leading to improved sleep and healthier eating choices.

Consult with your healthcare professional before starting a new exercise plan.

Reflection

Think about what behaviors you can implement to improve your physical health. Here are some examples.

- Take the stairs versus the elevator.

- Make multiple trips up and down stairs or outside your house to increase your steps.

- Park farther away from a building entrance.

- Treat more active chores, such as yardwork, as opportunities to exercise.

- Start a regular walking routine in the morning or in the evening.

Note behaviors you can do to improve your physical health.

_____

_____

_____

_____

HEALTHY EATING

I'm intentionally using the term *healthy eating* instead of the word *dieting*. The focus is on dealing with mindsets and feelings about food and eating that affect your choices. There are no prescriptive eating plans that are considered treatments for ADHD. Obviously, abide by any medical advice for managing food allergies and sensitivities, or medical issues like celiac disease, that are relevant to your health.

As always, specific, actionable plans have a better chance of working than broad, vague ones. One way to approach eating objectives is to have one healthy behavior you want to introduce or increase, and one unhealthy behavior you want to reduce or stop. For example, a positive action is to introduce a healthy snack option, such as grapes, and a corresponding reduction plan is to remove cookies from your house.

For healthy eating, your daily planner is a good tool for blocking out mealtimes. Your food options are tied to your food shopping behaviors and what items you select. Disorganization with food shopping may lead to excessive reliance on take-out or easy, but less healthy options. Time-management and implementation skills can be used to reduce overwhelm and sensory overload that some adults with ADHD face in grocery stores. Online grocery ordering and delivery options can be useful. Food-box subscriptions offer prepackaged healthy meal options. Unfortunately, some of these options can be expensive.

Meal prep can be taxing in terms of time and energy, though many people enjoy cooking. If daily meal choices and prep are stressful, you can devote a block of time, often on a weekend, for meal prep or menu planning for the week. This provides ready-made options during the week. You might rely on simple healthy meals with soup, a salad, and a sandwich. Regardless of your approach, precommitment reduces cognitive load and wasted time, effort, and energy.

Your beliefs and feelings about hunger and eating are important, too. Adults with ADHD are prone to impulsive, emotional, or stress eating (El Archi et al. 2020). Your thoughts and feelings often conspire to justify impulsive eating but for unfounded reasons (J. S. Beck 2008). To counteract this tendency, don't keep tempting foods in your home and be mindful of risky situations that can overwhelm self-control, like all-you-can-eat buffets.

When faced with food triggers, recognizing your feelings and bodily tells opens the door for coping via emotional labeling and the reminder that your actions are not dictated by these impulses. Just because that tasty treat on the baking show makes your mouth water doesn't mean you're hungry. This is how catching and assessing automatic thoughts and feelings and tolerating discomfort helps you delay the impulse so you can make informed choices.

Reflection

Here are some questions when facing cravings to help you navigate them.

Are you hungry for a meal, or were you triggered by a yummy-looking food?

_____

_____

_____

How does this food fit your healthy eating plan?

_____

_____

_____

Can you tolerate these feelings and delay the eating impulse for five minutes?

_____

_____

_____

Can you move away from the tempting situation?

_____

_____

_____

Can you exercise portion control if you choose to eat?

_____

_____

_____

How are your thoughts justifying eating the food? Is there another way to think this through?

_____

_____

_____

What is your "If _X_, then _Y_" implementation coping plan?

_____

_____

_____

There'll be times when you choose to eat something that's less healthy, such as a sweet treat. Just aim to keep it within reason. For example, portion control is a bounded eating task, such as limiting an ice cream portion to a small bowl. Tracking what you eat, for example, writing in a food diary or tracking meals in your planner, externalizes information that can give you ideas for healthier options. For instance, you may be inspired to add more fruits and vegetables to your meals.

If you're concerned that you may have a problem related to your eating behavior, talk to a healthcare professional.

Mealtimes are useful pivot points for other behaviors. For example, you can use dinnertime to habit-stack a walk afterward.

Downtime

Downtime is valuable real estate in your calendar. Downtime is whatever you do to rest, replenish, and clear your mind. Such endeavors need not be low key to reduce stress, though a degree of tranquility is not a bad thing. You might enjoy mindful relaxation, such as walking outside, reading a book, or practicing yoga. You might prefer active relaxation, such as running, bike riding, or rock climbing. Mind-engaging activities, such as watching a TED Talk or listening to podcasts, might be what regenerates you. It's whatever does the trick for you and affords peace of mind.

Reflection

List some downtime activities that give you peace of mind. Designating some downtime tasks helps give you a list to draw from when you feel like doing something but don't know what. Here are some examples:

- taking a nap

- reading for pleasure

- going for a walk or a bike ride

- sitting quietly

- going outside

- video gaming (Don't feel guilty if this is what you like, but practice portion control.)

- listening to music or playing an instrument

- doing a jigsaw puzzle

- solving crossword or sudoku puzzles

- snow or water skiing

- swimming

List some downtime activities that bring you piece of mind.

_____

_____

_____

_____

There'll be days when downtime is a limited resource, but hopefully finding enough of it keeps you balanced. Using phones and electronic gadgets is often a part of downtime, but this can be a mixed blessing, which we'll address next.

Your Relationship with Technology and Gadgets

Technology and electronic gadgets, for all their benefits, pose an ever-present means for escape-avoidance, particularly for adults with ADHD. What's more, even enjoying technology during downtime isn't necessarily a true respite. The tasks you are avoiding—chores, work projects, exercise—still burn mental energy by looming undone in your mind. This cognitive load disrupts our brain's circuitry, affecting both psychological and physical health (Levitin 2014; Paul 2021; Porges 2021) apart from ADHD.

Antiprocrastination plans can target technology or gadget use and help you decide whether they're necessary for tasks. If not essential to the task at hand, they're distractions to be kept out of reach and out of sight. When that's not possible, such as when using a computer for work, you need strategies to avoid temptation. For example, you can put your gadget in airplane mode to avoid going online. Implementation plans for what features you'll use and how you'll deal with temptations and slipups are tailor-made for such situations. ("If I catch myself online shopping, then I'll stop and reread the last paragraph.") You can also use distanced self-talk, coaching statements like "You can handle an hour studying before checking social media."

Urges to check gadgets, as with other impulses to escape, yield useful information about your view of tasks, namely feelings of stress or ugh. Predicting these potential emotions beforehand lends itself to antiprocrastination plans and strategies for what you'll do if you experience task-interfering feelings. Such escape-avoidance impulses often erupt when you approach a task. For example, you may justify checking your phone to get in the mood, or to reward yourself prematurely for getting any amount of work done (*I'm off to a good start. This feels good. I'll reward myself and check last night's scores*). Do these patterns sound familiar?

Such off-task drifts are tricky. Depending on how long you've been on task, such straying might signal the need for a break or maybe you've accomplished your objective and can stop. Such judgement calls require honest self-assessments and informed decisions. When wrapping up a task session for an ongoing project, such as a home renovation or writing assignment, it's good practice to schedule your next work session.

Breaks are sensitive pivot points. A bounded break is a helpful way to get you back on task after a break. As with task-bounding, your break is time-bound or task-bound, such as ten minutes or a cup of coffee, respectively, each offering hard stops. An implementation plan for getting back on task helps, too.

Reflection

In the spirit of the SAP plan and its specific, actionable steps (or don't-do steps) at targeted pivot points for technology and gadgets, here are some ideas to experiment with. Focus on progress, not perfection.

- Keep your phone out of reach, such as in your pocket or a drawer and practice delays in checking it when doing other things. (You can set unique ringtones for calls from a child's school or others you must answer.)

- If you're meeting with a group, remember the benefits of eye contact with others, even if you can hear and repeat what is said. That skill doesn't fulfill the social role of active listening.

- Use an old-school alarm clock instead of a phone to wake up.

- Log out of social media and other accounts to add the hassle of logging in each time to reduce checking.

- Use your device with a plan. This idea is like a bounded task combined with distanced self-talk. For example, you might check the status of a shopping order and then put your phone away.

- Have gadget-free times with family and friends (or on your own), such as during meals or while playing board games.

Make a list of specific, actionable steps to better manage the time you spend with technology.

_____

_____

_____

_____

All the health and well-being issues reviewed thus far represent implementation challenges familiar to most adults with ADHD. The next section briefly reviews other complexities that many adults with ADHD face and which you might need specialized support for.

Other Complexities That Affect Well-Being

Anxiety is the most common emotional ride-along for adults with ADHD, but there are other mental and physical health complications you may also be dealing with. These might require specialized care that takes into account how ADHD affects your life. Let's look at some examples.

Depression and Mood Disorders

Depression runs neck-and-neck with anxiety in terms of the foremost emotional issues in adult ADHD. Depression and anxiety often coexist. Whereas the theme of anxiety is facing risk and uncertainty, in depression it's loss. Such losses include opportunities and relationships, or a diminished sense of self, which ADHD can influence. In addition to emotional symptoms, such as self-criticism and hopelessness, physical symptoms of depression can make it harder to do things. Even if you're functional, life can be harder and less satisfying. Thoughts about suicide are a common symptom of depression. There is established evidence of suicide risk in adults with ADHD and mood problems (Barkley 2015).

Adult ADHD is associated with more failure experiences, which stoke depressed mood and pessimism. Insidiously, the ADHD-depression connection and escape-avoidance bring about more failures in a vicious cycle (Knouse, Zvorsky, and Safren 2013).

There are many effective antidepressant medications that can help stabilize mood, many of which can be prescribed alongside ADHD medications. CBT was originally designed to treat depression (A. T. Beck 1967), and many CBT strategies in this workbook can be used to improve mood.

If you are concerned that you may be suffering from depression, consult a healthcare professional.

Anxiety-Related Conditions

Here are some anxiety-related conditions adults with ADHD may experience.

- **Generalized anxiety** is the most prominent anxiety-related condition with ADHD. Various worries stem from the experiences of living with adult ADHD.

- **Panic disorder** is another anxiety disorder. Panic attacks are defined by a sudden, alarming tsunami of anxiety. This is a false alarm of the fight-or-flight system that can leave sufferers worried they're having a heart attack or losing control.

- **Social anxiety** is characterized by convictions that others will be judgmental and critical to the degree that social situations are avoided, including eating in restaurants or conversing with unfamiliar people.

- **Simple phobias** are feared reactions to specific situations or things, such as animals (snakes), the natural environment (heights, storms), blood-injection injury (needles), or settings (airplanes).

Although not classified as anxiety disorders, post-traumatic stress disorder (PTSD) and obsessive-compulsive disorder (OCD) can co-occur with ADHD. PTSD manifests as chronic trauma-based symptoms, such as flashbacks and reliving trauma reactions from experiencing or witnessing potential or actual harm to yourself or someone else, such as a rape, car accident, or natural disaster. OCD involves recurring, intrusive thoughts that are deemed "bad," often combined with repetitive, ritualized behaviors (including mental rituals) to neutralize them, such as excessive checking, that are quite impairing.

CBT-oriented treatment protocols exist for each of these mental health conditions and are highly effective. They share an emphasis on exposure and facing fears to learn more adaptive ways to deal with them, thereby overcoming the fear-based physical reactions and mindsets (Rosqvist 2005). Medications also can be helpful.

If you are concerned that you may be suffering from one of these mental health conditions, consult a healthcare professional.

Substance-Use Problems

There is an increased risk for substance-use problems among individuals with a history of ADHD, especially when untreated (Barkley 2015). Nicotine, marijuana, and alcohol are the main culprits. Extreme technology use and gaming might reach the realm of addiction for some individuals with ADHD and are certainly problematic for many.

Substance use might range from social, recreational use to abuse or dependence. Treatments are modified for the specific drug and level of problematic use. Inpatient rehabilitation programs for people struggling with dependence remove them from drug availability to establish stability and recovery. There are intensive outpatient programs with multiple treatment sessions per week, often augmented with 12-step programs.

If you are concerned that you may be struggling with substance abuse, consult a health care professional.

Medical Problems

It's increasingly apparent that a personal history of ADHD presents risks for physical and medical health issues in adulthood (Barkley and Fischer 2019). Poor time management and disorganization interfere with scheduling preventative checkups and compliance with prescribed regimens, such as diabetes management. Keeping up with prescriptions and follow-up appointments is challenging for adults with ADHD. A task-based view lends itself to organization and follow-through on healthy behaviors and keeping up with healthcare appointments. As ADHD is an implementation problem, improving medical health habits is a worthwhile aim of medical and nonmedical treatments for adult ADHD.

Summary

This chapter focused on using active coping of the sort you've learned in this workbook to leverage your strengths and improve your self-care. Remember to cheer yourself on for the steps forward that you're taking. Even small gains in health and well-being reduce stress and anxiety and promote overall well-being and better ADHD management. Chapter 9 will wrap up the workbook on a high note to keep you motivated as you move ahead.

This End Can Be a New Beginning

This chapter is both the end of this workbook and the beginning of using what you've learned in your daily life. The workbook is an ever-ready resource for you, much like a cookbook. However, the recipes are now yours. By this I mean that, extending the cookbook and recipe analogies, you're seasoning the coping strategies and ideas to your circumstances and to your style and tastes. Everyday cooking requires flexibility. You might run out of ingredients and need to improvise using what's available, cater to others' dietary needs, or simply decide to go off-recipe and try something new.

This chapter takes a long view of coping with ADHD. It will touch on issues that accompany positive change, including stress. It'll also serve as a booster if you start to drift from coping plans or doubt yourself, so that you can get back on track.

New Challenges

Rehabilitation in healthcare reflects efforts to restore a previous level of functioning, or as close as possible, such as physical rehabilitation after surgery. *Habilitation* represents efforts to normalize your existing functioning to optimize your skills, perhaps adding new ones to your repertoire. An aspirational view of CBT for adult ADHD is that it fosters what I call *abilitation:* transcending problems, acquiring skills to pursue new ventures (or picking up ones that had been set aside), and seeking opportunities for growth and flourishing (Ramsay and Rostain 2015b).

On the one hand, positive psychology highlights the flourishing and gifts often attributed to features of adult ADHD. On the other hand, many adults with ADHD are dispirited by ongoing life struggles, being unable to claim any discernible superpowers from ADHD. The toxic positivity from social media provides more fodder for their negative comparisons and frustration. I recall a social media posting asking, "If ADHD is a gift, can I return it?"

Both views deserve consideration. Reading this workbook, some readers might be inspired to finish an incomplete college course, sign up for a certification program, or pursue a passion, such as an art class. Others may achieve comparable triumphs by keeping on top of chores or their job duties more reliably, or improving their self-care, for example, by having more downtime for themselves. Both are examples of thriving. Be on guard that the latter examples can be easily dismissed by discounting the positive: *This is what I should have been doing all along.* Yet, this is one of the takeaways from this chapter: identify and honor your authentic improvements, especially incremental ones like doing better than you were before you picked up this workbook.

Reflection

What are some authentic, incremental improvements you've noticed using the coping strategies and exercises in this workbook, even if they're still insights and ideas from working through the exercises at this point?

_____

_____

_____

_____

_____

_____

_____

_____

Practice

You can celebrate incremental progress without having reached your desired goal yet. See if any of these mindsets look familiar. For each one, write an adaptive coping answer, maybe using a distanced self-talk *you* message.

Comparative thinking: *I'm still not doing this as well as* _____. (Fill in the blank, such as a name of someone like a coworker or a general example, such as "others using this book.")

_____

_____

_____

Should statement (comparison with an unrealistic standard): *I should be doing better by now" or "I should be able to do this without a workbook by this point in my life.*

_____

_____

_____

Discounting the positive: *I did well with the skills for a while, but I slipped over the weekend. I should've known I wouldn't change.*

_____

_____

_____

All-or-nothing thinking: *If I miss a day using my planner or I procrastinate, then this isn't working.*

_____

_____

_____

_____

With the skills learned in this workbook, you can continue to make and recognize incremental improvements when faced with new challenges. You'll likely also start to expect more from yourself. For example, you might be on time for meetings more consistently, but then a missed appointment feels especially disheartening. Normalizing and acknowledging slipups, reverse engineering and fixing them, and practicing self-compassion—including recognizing that this stress is a sign you're improving—are all facets of good coping.

Framing coping issues in behavioral terms is another strategy for resilient coping. Using behavioral language can be an effective strategy when communicating with others, such as with friends and coworkers, about your behavior—and theirs, at times. For example, Kelly let a coworker know that their supposed good-natured teasing bothered her by saying: "When you refer to 'Kelly time,' I feel embarrassed. I'd like it if you didn't do that anymore."

Kelly's example is a reminder of the highly personal nature of ADHD. Executive functions are intimately involved in what you set out to do. Endeavors are often associated with your sense of self. Consequently, you can be your own harshest critic, the opposite of practicing self-compassion. But rebooting your coping efforts with the SAP plan of specific, actionable behaviors implemented at targeted pivot points makes bouncing back more manageable. It's not necessarily easy, but easier than trying to change your character.

Reflection

What are some self-criticisms or others' criticisms about ADHD-related issues that you can define as specific behaviors to address? Do any of the following seem familiar?

- Late arrivals

- Forgetting meetings or promises made to others

- Procrastination or other escape-avoidance

- Lateness with work or assignments

- Handling feedback from others

- Emotional overreactions

Note any other similar behaviors.

_____

_____

_____

In addition to being mindful of unhelpful self-talk, you might have emotional reactions to slipups and criticisms, especially after making progress, and worries that you'll regress. As before, recognize and label the triggers, thoughts, and feelings or sensations. These distancing steps provide emotional and mental space for you to work with and through your emotions. Remember, even unpleasant reactions often reveal positive attributes, such as wanting to be on time and to keep promises. You can affirm these strengths while keeping your emotions proportional to your slipup.

Don't forget that these issues will arise because you're doing better, which is a good problem to have. But it's authentic. Just as positive change raises expectations, it also opens the door for new opportunities, which we'll discuss next.

New Opportunities

A guiding idea in CBT is to make the therapist obsolete. The skills belong to you to use as you like. Still, many people continue with periodic CBT booster sessions or return for a few tune-up meetings when facing newfound challenges, like a new job.

To this end, you have this workbook and online materials, which you can access at http://www.newharbinger.com/52434, as a reference to dog-ear and mark up with notes or digital equivalents. You might pursue other supports for managing ADHD to further your abilitation path. These last pages provide an opportunity for blue-sky thinking about things you want to do and how you want to spend your time.

You might have picked up this workbook with some big ideas already percolating. You might also have some small stuff, day-to-day objectives, such as keeping up with chores or regularly using a planner, which are equally noble intentions. Then again, such foundational strategies can support broader undertakings and goals. Let's consider your plans.

Reflection

Below are some prompts to consider ways you can use your skills to turn intentions into actions.

What are some of your rehabilitation goals? These could be projects or habits that worked well in the past or that you dropped and you'd like to revisit.

_____

_____

_____

_____

What are some of your habilitation goals? These are the understandings you've gained about yourself and how you can arrange circumstances to set yourself up for success. Examples might be the ways you modified the recipes for the workbook coping strategies to work better for you.

_____

_____

_____

_____

What are some of your abilitation goals—projects, endeavors, or goals that you might have assumed you couldn't do or even try but that you might consider now?

_____

_____

_____

_____

_____

What are other habits, duties, adult roles, relationships, or personal goals for which you'd like to turn intentions into actions?

_____

_____

_____

_____

_____

_____

Even positive change is stressful. Your CBT skills will help you manage the various forms of stress and ADHD anxiety you'll experience when pursuing old or new goals. Don't forget that some stress is motivating, and sensations associated with positive excitement and curiosity resemble those of nervous apprehension, like _I'm anxious for my first adult ADHD support group meeting._

Externalizing information and motivation to keep your intentions and valuation at the front of your brain helps with follow-through. Your planner, antiprocrastination plan, and motivational reminders will also keep you on track. When in doubt, your cognitive skills will help you generate a coping mindset, buoyed by distanced self-talk for task initiation and emotion management (Kross 2021). Implementation statements are a go-to for launching the first behavioral step in any plan (Gollwitzer and Oettingen 2016), as is the SAP plan.

Practice

Record motivational, inspirational reminders and quotes that you'll use to follow through on your goals. You can add new ones that you discover along the way. In this way, this book will really be yours, which is a great way to wrap up.

_____

_____

_____

_____

_____

_____

_____

_____

_____

_____

_____

_____

_____

Summary

Well done, you! You've done a lot. You learned about ADHD, anxiety, and contemporary understandings of what they are and how to see them so that you can do something about them. This led to a discussion of their special connection, the combination of consistent inconsistency and the uncertainty the underlies the adult ADHD–anxiety connection.

We covered the CBT model adapted to adult ADHD and how you can use it to dismantle the adult ADHD–anxiety connection. You practiced noticing and reevaluating your thoughts, feelings, and actions; forming implementation plans for your intentions; and considering the ripple effects of ADHD through your social networks. You used this framework to work through your potential skepticism and doubts about the planner and other coping skills.

You waded through chapters on time-management and antiprocrastination skills and strategies to better manage executive-function problems and better organize and implement your intentions.

A significant topic was your social life and how ADHD affects relationships and your social domains. You can use the analogy of social capital to help manage your relationship accounts and self-advocate, including promoting self-compassion and avoiding toxic relationships.

We spent a chapter looking at health and well-being issues that affect and are affected by the adult ADHD–anxiety connection. Healthy habits and self-care most certainly support better coping with ADHD and will reduce your stress.

Lastly, we reviewed a few challenges and the many more opportunities that come with your progress. The coping strategies for managing ADHD provide a foundation for you to build consistent consistency. Even though life with ADHD involves uncertainty, you have the requisite tools to turn your intentions into actions and realize your plans and goals.

I used recipes and cooking as examples illustrating the connection of small steps for realizing larger-later, highly desired goals. This is the recipe that culminates in a tasty dish. I hope you feel that this book spoke to you and your adult ADHD–anxiety connection. I hope you were able to personalize the book and create your own recipes and, mostly, that you now trust your ability to implement them. Now get cooking!

References

2018 Physical Activity Guidelines Advisory Committee. 2018. *2018 Physical Activity Guidelines Advisory Committee Scientific Report.* Washington, DC: US Department of Health and Human Services.

Bandura, A. 1997. *Self-Efficacy: The Exercise of Control.* New York: Freeman.

Barkley, R. A. 2012. *Executive Functions: What They Are, How They Work, and Why They Evolved.* New York: Guilford Press.

————. 2015. *Attention-Deficit Hyperactivity Disorder: A Handbook for Diagnosis and Treatment*, 4th ed. New York: Guilford Press.

Barkley, R. A., and M. Fischer. 2019. "Hyperactive Childhood Syndrome and Estimated Life Expectancy at Young Adult Follow-Up: The Role of Adult ADHD and Other Potential Predictors." *Journal of Attention Disorders* 23: 907–923.

Barrett, L. F., J. Gross, T. C. Christensen, and M. Benvenuto. 2001. "Knowing What You're Feeling and Knowing What to Do About It: Mapping the Relation Between Emotion Differentiation and Emotion Regulation." *Cognition and Emotion* 15: 713–724.

Beaton, D. M., F. Sirois, and E. Milne. 2020. "Self-Compassion and Perceived Criticism in Adults with Attention Deficit Hyperactivity Disorder (ADHD)." *Mindfulness* 11: 2506–2518.

————. 2022. "The Role of Self-Compassion in the Mental Health of Adults with ADHD." *Journal of Clinical Psychology* 78(12): 2497–2512.

Beck, A. T. 1967. *Depression: Causes and Treatments.* Philadelphia: University of Pennsylvania Press.

Beck, A. T., G. Emery, and R. L. Greenberg. 1985. *Anxiety Disorders and Phobias: A Cognitive Perspective.* New York: Basic Books.

Beck, J. S. 2008. *The Beck Diet Solution.* Birmingham, AL: Oxmoor House.

Bodalski, E. A., L. E. Knouse, and D. Kovalev. 2019. "Adult ADHD, Emotion Dysregulation, and Functional Outcomes: Examining the Role of Emotion Regulation Strategies." *Journal of Psychopathology and Behavioral Assessment* 41: 81–92.

Brooks, J. A., H. Shablack, M. Gendron, A. B. Satpute, M. H. Parrish, and K. A. Lindquist. 2017. "The Role of Language in the Experience and Perception of Emotion: A Neuroimaging Meta-Analysis." *Social Cognitive and Affective Neuroscience* 12: 169–183.

Brown, T. A., T. A. O'Leary, and D. H. Barlow. 2001. "Generalized Anxiety Disorder." In *Clinical Handbook of Psychological Disorders,* 3rd ed., edited by D. H. Barlow. New York: Guilford Press.

Burns, D. D. 2020. *Feeling Great: The Revolutionary New Treatment for Depression and Anxiety.* Eau Claire, WI: PESI.

Children and Adults with Attention-Deficit/Hyperactivity Disorder (CHADD). 2015. "Fact Sheet: ADHD and Comorbidities." *CHADD.*

Chung, W., S.-F. Jiang, D. Paksarian, A. Nikolaidis, F. X. Castellanos, K. R. Merikangas, and M. P. Milham. 2019. "Trends in the Prevalence and Incidence of Attention-Deficit/Hyperactivity Disorder Among Adults and Children of Different Racial and Ethnic Groups." *JAMA Network Open* 2(11): e1914344.

Dodson, W. 2023. "How ADHD Ignites Rejection Sensitive Dysphoria." *Additude Magazine.* https://www.additudemag.com/rejection-sensitive-dysphoria-and-adhd.

Dugas, M. J., F. Gagnon, R. Ladouceur, and M. H. Freeston. 1998. "Generalized Anxiety Disorder: A Preliminary Test of a Conceptual Model." *Behaviour Research and Therapy* 36(2): 215–226.

Duhigg, C. 2012. *The Power of Habit: Why We Do What We Do in Life and Business.* New York: Random House.

El Archi, S., S. Cortese, N. Ballon, C. Réveillère, A. De Luca, S. Barrault, and P. Brunault. 2020. "Negative Affectivity and Emotional Dysregulation as Mediators Between ADHD and Disordered Eating: A Systematic Review." *Nutrients* 12(11): 3292.

Fuller-Thomson, E., L. Carrique, and A. MacNeil. 2022. "Generalized Anxiety Disorder Among Adults with Attention Deficit Hyperactivity Disorder." *Journal of Affective Disorders* 299: 707–714.

Goldstein, S., and J. A. Naglieri, eds. 2014. *Handbook of Executive Functioning.* New York: Springer.

Gollwitzer, P. M., and G. Oettingen. 2016. "Planning Promotes Goal Striving." In *Handbook of Self-Regulation: Research, Theory, and Applications,* 3rd ed., edited by K. D. Vohs and R. F. Baumeister. New York: Guilford Press.

Guntuku, S. C., J. R. Ramsay, R. M. Merchant, and L. H. Ungar. 2019. "Language of ADHD in Adults on Social Media." *Journal of Attention Disorders* 23: 1475–1485.

Haidt, J. 2006. *The Happiness Hypothesis: Finding Modern Truth in Ancient Wisdom.* New York: Basic Books.

Hallowell, E. M. 1997. *Worry: Hope and Help for a Common Condition.* New York: Random House.

Hallowell, E. M., and J. J. Ratey. 2021. *ADHD 2.0: New Science and Essential Strategies for Thriving with Distraction—From Childhood Through Adulthood.* New York: Ballantine Books.

Hinshaw, S. P., P. T. Nguyen, S. M. O'Grady, and E. A. Rosenthal. 2022. "Annual Research Review: Attention-Deficit/Hyperactivity Disorder in Girls and Women: Underrepresentation, Longitudinal Process, and Key Directions." *Journal of Child Psychology and Psychiatry* 63(4): 484–496.

Hofmann, S. G. 2016. *Emotion in Therapy: From Science to Practice.* New York: Guilford Press.

Jaffe, E. 2013. "Why Wait? The Science Behind Procrastination." *APS Observer,* March 29. www.psychologicalscience.org/observer/why-wait-the-science-behind-procrastination.

Kelly, K., and P. Ramundo. 1993. *You Mean I'm Not Lazy, Stupid, or Crazy?!* New York: Scribner.

Knouse, L. E., I. Zvorsky, and S. A. Safren. 2013. "Depression in Adults with Attention-Deficit/Hyperactivity Disorder (ADHD): The Mediating Role of Cognitive-Behavioral Factors." *Cognitive Therapy & Research* 37: 1220–1232.

Kross, E. 2021. *Chatter: The Voice in Our Head, Why It Matters, and How to Harness It.* New York: Crown.

Leahy, R. L. 2005. *The Worry Cure: Seven Steps to Stop Worry from Stopping You.* New York: Guilford Press.

Leary, M. R., C. Springer, L. Negel, E. Ansell, and K. Evans. 1998. "The Causes, Phenomenology, and Consequences of Hurt Feelings." *Journal of Personality and Social Psychology* 74(5): 1225–1237.

Levitin, D. J. 2014. *The Organized Mind: Thinking Straight in the Age of Information Overload.* New York: Plume.

Lieberman, M. D., N. I. Eisenberger, M. J. Crockett, S. M. Tom, J. H. Pfeifer, and B. M. Way. 2007. "Putting Feeling into Words: Affect Labeling Disrupts Amygdala Activity in Response to Affective Stimuli." *Psychological Science* 18: 421–428.

Lokuge, S., K. Fotinos, S. Clarissa, C. Bains, T. Sternat, I. Epstein, et al. 2023. "Underlying Mechanisms of ADHD Predict Anxiety Severity: A Preliminary Analysis Paper." Presented at The Annual Conference of the American Professional Society of ADHD and Related Disorders, Orlando, FL.

Mlodinow, L. 2022. *Emotional: How Feelings Shape Our Thinking.* New York: Pantheon.

Orlov, M. 2010. *The ADHD Effect on Marriage: Understand and Rebuild Your Relationship in Six Steps.* Plantation, FL: Specialty Press.

Paul, A. M. 2021. *The Extended Mind: The Power of Thinking Outside the Brain.* New York: Houghton Mifflin Harcourt.

Pera, G. 2008. *Is It You, Me, or Adult A.D.D.? Stopping the Roller Coaster When Someone You Love Has Attention Deficit Disorder.* San Francisco, CA: 1201 Alarm Press.

Pera, G., and A. L. Robin, eds. 2016. *Adult ADHD-Focused Couple Therapy: Clinical Interventions.* New York: Routledge.

Peterson, C., and M. E. P. Seligman. 2004. *Character Strengths and Virtues: A Handbook and Classification.* Washington, DC: American Psychological Association.

Porges, S. W., ed. 2021. *Polyvagal Safety: Attachment, Communication, Self-Regulation.* New York: W. W. Norton.

Ramsay, J. R. 2020. *Rethinking Adult ADHD: Helping Clients Turn Intentions into Actions.* Washington, DC: American Psychological Association.

Ramsay, J. R., and A. L. Rostain. 2015a. *The Adult ADHD Tool Kit: Using CBT to Facilitate Coping Inside and Out.* New York: Routledge.

———. 2015b. *Cognitive Behavioral Therapy for Adult ADHD: An Integrative Psychosocial and Medical Approach.* 2nd ed. New York: Routledge.

————. 2016. "Adult ADHD as an Implementation Problem: Clinical Significance, Underlying Mechanisms, and Psychosocial Treatment." *Practice Innovations* 1(1): 36–52.

Ratey, J. 2008. *Spark: The Revolutionary New Science of Exercise and the Brain.* New York: Little, Brown.

Roemer, L., E. H. Eustis, and S. M. Orsillo. 2021. "Generalized Anxiety Disorder: An Acceptance-Based Behavioral Therapy." In *Clinical Handbook of Psychological Disorders,* 5th ed., edited by D. H. Barlow. New York: Guilford Press.

Rogers, D. C., A. J. Dittner, K. A. Rimes, and T. Chalder. 2017. "Fatigue in an Adult Attention Deficit Hyperactivity Disorder Population: A Trans-Diagnostic Approach." *British Journal of Clinical Psychology* 56: 33–52.

Rosenfield, B., J. R. Ramsay, and A. L. Rostain. 2008. "Extreme Makeover: The Case of a Young Adult Man with Severe Attention-Deficit/Hyperactivity Disorder." *Clinical Case Studies* 7(6): 471–490.

Rosqvist, J. 2005. *Exposure Treatments for Anxiety Disorders: A Practitioner's Guide to Concepts, Methods, and Evidence-Based Practice.* New York: Routledge.

Sarkis, S. M. 2018. *Gaslighting: Recognize Manipulative and Emotionally Abusive People—and Break Free.* New York: De Capo Press.

————. 2022. *Healing from Toxic Relationships: 10 Essential Steps to Recover from Gaslighting, Narcissism, and Emotional Abuse.* New York: Hachette.

Sedgwick, J. A., A. Merwood, and P. Asherson. 2019. "The Positive Aspects of Attention Deficit Hyperactivity Disorder: A Qualitative Investigation of Successful Adults with ADHD." *ADHD Attention Deficit Hyperactivity Disorder* 11: 241–253.

Seligman, M. E. P., and M. Csikszentmihalyi. 2000. "Positive Psychology: An Introduction." *American Psychologist* 55(1): 5–14.

Spradlin, S. E. 2003. *Don't Let Your Emotions Run Your Life: How Dialectical Behavior Therapy Can Put You in Control.* Oakland, CA: New Harbinger.

Steel, P. 2007. "The Nature of Procrastination: A Meta-Analytic and Theoretical Review of Quintessential Self-Regulatory Failure." *Psychological Bulletin* 133(1): 65–94.

Strohmeier, C., B. Rosenfield, R. A. DiTomasso, and J. R. Ramsay. 2016. "Assessment of the Relationship Between Cognitive Distortions, Adult ADHD, Anxiety, Depression, and Hopelessness." *Psychiatry Research* 238: 153–158.

Surman, C. B. H., and D. M. Walsh. 2022. "Do Treatments for Adult ADHD Improve Emotional Behavior? A Systematic Review and Analysis." *Journal of Attention Disorders* 26(14): 1822–1832.

Tierney, J., and R. F. Baumeister. 2019. *The Power of Bad: How the Negativity Effect Rules Us and How We Can Rule It.* New York: Penguin.

Wright, R. 1994. *The Moral Animal: Evolutionary Psychology and Everyday Life.* New York: Vintage Books.

Young, J. L. 2013. "Chronic Fatigue Syndrome: 3 Cases and a Discussion of the Natural History of Attention-Deficit/Hyperactivity Disorder." *Postgraduate Medicine* 125: 162–168.

J. Russell Ramsay, PhD, ABPP, is a licensed psychologist specializing in the assessment and psychosocial treatment of adult attention deficit/hyperactive disorder (ADHD). Before embarking on his solo virtual practice, he was cofounder and clinical director of the University of Pennsylvania's Adult ADHD Treatment and Research Program, where he was professor of clinical psychology in psychiatry. Ramsay is widely published, including five books on adult ADHD; lectures internationally and virtually; and is in the Children and Adults with Attention-Deficit/Hyperactivity Disorder (CHADD) Hall of Fame. He is from the Greater Philadelphia, PA, area.

Foreword writer **Ari Tuckman, PsyD,** is a clinical psychologist in private practice in West Chester, PA, specializing in the diagnosis and treatment of ADHD. He presents frequently on ADHD and related topics to both professionals and members of the public.

Real change *is* possible

For more than forty-five years, New Harbinger has published proven-effective self-help books and pioneering workbooks to help readers of all ages and backgrounds improve mental health and well-being, and achieve lasting personal growth. In addition, our spirituality books offer profound guidance for deepening awareness and cultivating healing, self-discovery, and fulfillment.

Founded by psychologist Matthew McKay and Patrick Fanning, New Harbinger is proud to be an independent, employee-owned company. Our books reflect our core values of integrity, innovation, commitment, sustainability, compassion, and trust. Written by leaders in the field and recommended by therapists worldwide, New Harbinger books are practical, accessible, and provide real tools for real change.

 **newharbinger**publications

MORE BOOKS from
NEW HARBINGER PUBLICATIONS

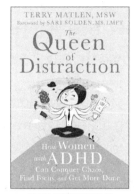

Did you know there are **free tools** you can download for this book?

Free tools are things like **worksheets**, **guided meditation exercises**, and **more** that will help you get the most out of your book.

You can download free tools for this book—whether you bought or borrowed it, in any format, from any source—from the New Harbinger website. All you need is a NewHarbinger.com account. Just use the URL provided in this book to view the free tools that are available for it. Then, click on the "download" button for the free tool you want, and follow the prompts that appear to log in to your NewHarbinger.com account and download the material.

You can also save the free tools for this book to your **Free Tools Library** so you can access them again anytime, just by logging in to your account! Just look for this button on the book's free tools page.

+ Save this to my free tools library

If you need help accessing or downloading free tools, visit **newharbinger.com/faq** or contact us at **customerservice@newharbinger.com**.